REINVENTING YOUR CITY

REINVENTING YOUR CITY

EIGHT STEPS TO TURN YOUR CITY AROUND

KIM J. BRIESEMEISTER & CHRISTOPHER J. BROWN

URBANITE PUBLISHING
POMPANO BEACH, FL

© 2015 Kim J. Briesemeister and Christopher J. Brown

All rights reserved. No part of this publication may be reproduced, stored in a retrieval system, or transmitted in any form or by any means electronic, mechanical, photocopying, recording or otherwise, without the prior written permission of the publisher.

Published by
Urbanite Publishing
Pompano Beach, FL

> Publisher's Cataloging-in-Publication Data
> Briesemeister, Kim J.
>
> Reinventing your city : eight steps to turn your city around / Kim J. Briesemeister & Christopher J. Brown.—Pompano Beach, FL : Urbanite Pub., 2015.
>
> p. ; cm.
>
> ISBN13: 978-0-9860860-0-7
>
> 1. City planning. 2. Community development, Urban. I. Title. II. Brown, Christopher J.
>
> HT166.B74 2015
> 307.1216—dc23   2015945301

FIRST EDITION

Project coordination by Jenkins Group, Inc.
www.BookPublishing.com

Interior design by Brooke Camfield

Printed in the United States of America
20 19 18 17 16 • 5 4 3 2 1

CONTENTS

	Prologue	vii
	Introduction	ix
1:	The Vision	1
2:	Leadership and Politics	17
3:	The Team	37
4:	The Plan	49
5:	Implementation	69
6:	Private Investment	97
7:	Financing Redevelopment	119
8:	Reinventing the City	127
	Some Conclusions	139
	Case Studies	143
	Bilbao, Spain	143
	Charleston, South Carolina	154
	Delray Beach, Florida	161
	The Hague, Netherlands	168
	Curacao, Dutch Caribbean	182
	Bibliography	195
	Credits	199
	About the Authors	201

PROLOGUE

What do you see when you drive around your city or walk your main street? Do you see abandoned buildings, shabby streetscapes and little or no pedestrian activity? Are you perplexed by what you see? Do you compare your city to other cities you have visited that have a thriving downtown, filled with restaurants and shops, and beautiful, walkable streets?

Often, while lecturing or making presentations about successful city redevelopment efforts, we are asked, "How does a city do it? How do you turn a city around?" We usually respond that you have to start with a very clear vision, and you need to find one or more leaders to carry out and protect the vision.

We realized that the "process" of turning a city around isn't always obvious, and more importantly, that there are certain steps that must be followed.

So, instead of just writing about what makes a great city, we decided to write about the critical and key steps that every city goes through during its transformation. These steps are not only critical; they make the difference between cities that are successful at transformation and those that languish. While we do still talk about elements of a great city, the emphasis is on the process. We simply named it "Eight Steps to Turn Your City Around."

We also recognized that while each city has its own unique characteristics and issues, there is a definite pattern or series of events that have taken place in cities that were able to transform themselves into thriving communities with a clear brand that people want to be associated with, regardless of what continent they are on.

Our work has taken us to over eighty cities worldwide. Even in the far reaches of Europe, the Caribbean, and South American lands, the people we interviewed all reiterated, without our prompting, the same basic steps that made them successful. The need for change in cities usually starts with some form of a crisis, where the city is facing issues so challenging that it has to do something about them.

We have been fortunate enough to have worked in many of these cities from the beginning of the process all the way through to some form of success. The process for reinvention can run for as long as twenty-five years. Some cities are so desperate to see something happen immediately they cause their own demise because they look for the silver bullet and skip some critical steps. There is no quick fix. Transformation takes decades, after which, the leaders of the city must reconvene with their citizens to talk about a new long term vision.

This book is about how to define the vision, find a leader, make a plan based upon the vision, assemble the right team of highly skilled implementers, finance the effort, get the private sector to invest in the vision, and work very hard for the years it takes to make a great city.

Included are examples of several cities that we have worked with on reinvention and the things those cities did that made the difference in what they are today. We have both lived abroad, so we included international examples from cities we either lived in or worked in, or that fascinated us enough to include as great examples, such as Charleston, South Carolina; Bilbao, Spain; The Hague, Netherlands; and Curacao in the Dutch Caribbean.

We hope this book helps create the right conversation for your city to begin taking the eight steps to a successful reinvention, or to simply become a better city.

Christopher J. Brown and Kim J. Briesemeister
July 1, 2015

INTRODUCTION

Chicago, 2012. Robert Novak, a financial analyst, and his wife, Ana, a school teacher, both over sixty, were sitting at their breakfast table discussing an upcoming two-week vacation. Where to go was the topic. They wanted to travel to a place that had great food, museums, places to walk, friendly locals and young people. It also had to be in a pleasant environment and contain elements of history. They wanted to be in an urban locale and not be dependent upon an automobile. They made a list of cities in the United States that met some of these requirements. Here is their partial list: Brooklyn, New York; Charleston, South Carolina; Savannah, Georgia; Delray Beach, Florida; Miami Beach, Florida; West Palm Beach, Florida; and, Sarasota, Florida. They narrowed their choice to Delray Beach or West Palm Beach. These two cities have day and night life, museums, theaters, a main street, places to walk, young people and boomers living downtown, historical places, local transportation, small boutiques for shopping, outdoor cafes and great restaurants. In the end, the Novaks chose Delray Beach. The Novaks enjoyed their trip and felt welcomed by the city. One year later, the Novaks made Delray Beach their new home.

What makes great cities? The following is the Novaks' list:

Downtown Attributes

	Delray/ West Palm Beach	Brooklyn	Charleston	Sarasota
Main Street	Yes	Yes	Yes	Yes
Good Street Walking	Yes	Yes	Yes	Yes
Beautiful Public Plaza	Yes	Yes (park)	Yes (park)	Yes (park)
Places to Meet People	Yes	Yes	Yes	Yes
Cultural Facilities	Yes	Yes	Yes	Yes (many)
Unique Shopping	Yes	Yes (many)	Yes	Yes
Local Transportation	Yes (trolley)	Yes	City Bus	City Bus
Clean Downtown	Yes	Transitioning	Yes	Yes
Coffee Shops	Yes	Yes	Yes	Yes
Green Market	Yes	Yes	Unknown	Yes
Juice Bar	Yes	Yes	Yes	No
Yoga Studio	Yes	Yes	Unknown	Yes
Outdoor Café(s)	Yes (many)	Yes	Yes (few)	Yes
Nightlife with Music	Yes (many)	Yes	Yes	Yes
Great Restaurants	Yes (many)	Yes (many)	Yes (many)	Yes
Young People	Yes	Yes (many)	Yes	No
Cool Factor	Yes	Yes (high)	Yes	Yes
Friendly Locals	Yes	Maybe	Yes	Maybe
Great Hotels	Yes	Few	Yes	Yes
Great Weather	Yes	Seasonal	Sometimes	Yes

Why are we drawn to these kinds of cities? Why do we find ourselves in European cities such as Florence on our vacations? Why do we often pick our retirement city from a list similar to that made by the Novaks?

If the mayor of West Palm Beach, Florida, were to make a list of important qualities in great cities, she would probably agree with the Novaks, but would likely add the following:

- Strong tax base
- Financial reserves
- Great city services
- Respectful, educated, friendly city employees
- An engaged city
- A vibrant downtown
- A green city
- Diversified economy
- Good assistance to lower-income citizens and neighborhoods
- Facilities for children
- Parks in every neighborhood

Once the Novaks decided they could work out of their home and leave Chicago, they added the following to their list:

- Educational institutions for continuing education
- Historical society
- Music classes

The Novaks' and the mayor's lists are goals for almost every city mayor. In the 1980s and 1990s, Delray Beach and West Palm Beach, respectively, both convened committees for the purpose of addressing their blighted, vacant, ugly, money-losing downtowns. These cities were in crisis. Their unified response, as it has been for many cities nationwide, was "redevelopment." Why redevelopment? How do you get rid of blight? How do you get started and what are the steps? The answers can be found in this book. It's about vision, it's about the leadership and politics needed to implement the vision, it's about who's in place and on the team, it's about the plan, and it's about having all the right ingredients in place to remake and shape a great city.

How did West Palm Beach and Delray Beach turn their respective cities around? Having worked in both cities and many others, our experience has taught us there are eight steps, that if followed, will result in reinventing a city. Turning your city around, therefore, can be accomplished by doing the following:

I. Creating a vision
II. Identifying the leader
III. Assembling the core team
IV. Developing a plan
V. Implementing the plan
VI. Engaging the private sector
VII. Financing the plan
VIII. Starting the reinvention cycle again

Abandoned Old School Square, 1985. Delray Beach, Florida

The cities that we studied have a number of factors in common. There was the essential, political consensus to turn their cities around.

Having a crisis in a city motivates elected officials to focus on reinvention. The elected officials in Delray Beach and West Palm Beach witnessed an ever-decreasing tax base and a significantly progressive shabby transformation of the city. Their crises were part financial, and part physical. An additional crisis for both cities was a noticeable rise in crime.

The politicians began articulating a set of general visions, followed by more specific ideas spelled out in a detailed plan.

Once plans were developed, Delray Beach and West Palm Beach spent years implementing their plans. Both of these cities took a leap of faith. They invested millions in turning their cities around. The results, as we discuss throughout the book, more than justified the risk, the investment and the commitment to change. This book is about reinventing your city—how you do it, how to get started and how to be successful.

THE VISION

RE Inventing your city begins with a vision of what you want your city to become. Creating this vision is the first step to reinvention. Everyone knows a blighted or dilapidated area when they see one. In fact, most people feel instinctively unsafe when they drive through an area that has poor lighting, or that looks run down. Everything from broken windows on a building to graffiti-laden street signs can signal an area that lacks community pride and investment. Sometimes areas have been blighted or have lacked attention for so long that they become status quo and get nicknames like "the hood," or "the boulevard." When areas get really bad, some organizations can't help but identify these cities and put them on lists, like *Forbes'* list of *The 10 Most Dangerous U.S. Cities*, or RealEstatemsn.com's *10 Miserable Cities*. These are monikers that would make any mayor cringe and that also create residents' despair.

Then, there's the less-onerous scenario where total chaos and crime aren't the issue, but for some reason, these cities get passed over when big real estate markets come along. During the real estate boom that started in 2000 and ran through 2006, some cities thrived while others plodded along and fell into the abyss that led to the great recession. Why did some cities miss out, even when there was so much real estate investment going on?

The areas or cities that stay blighted, the ones that miss the real estate investment cycles, and the ones that seem to never get any attention, simply lack a vision. They can't define it, they don't portray it, and they certainly don't have a documented and clear path that points everyone in the same direction toward that vision.

The big question is then, "How does a city clearly identify the right vision?"

We all know cities that have clearly defined their vision, or at least defined what they don't want to be known for. Las Vegas is NOT a bedroom community, and Charleston, South Carolina, is NOT a twenty-four-hour city that never sleeps.

Finding Your City's Hidden Assets

One of the most interesting things about the reinvention of an area is that very often, it isn't until AFTER an area has been redeveloped and comes into its own that people recognize the components of what made the change occur. Too often, the city council or commissioners don't know where to start and can't "see the vision" themselves. They hire consultant after consultant to draw up plans and wonder why still nothing happens. "Why aren't the developers coming to our town?" the city manager of Oakland Park, in South Florida, lamented when we met with him. He said, "We did everything right! We hired a land planning firm and created a master plan! We spent $13 million on new streets and parking! Businesses aren't opening! No one is investing and I don't know why!!"

In Oakland Park's case, it was simply the lack of a clearly defined vision for the city.

The streets were nice. The parking was nice, albeit unused. But the plan they created didn't identify what the vision for the area should be to truly give it an identity that businesses and developers could connect with. To help this city identify their own special niche, we started with the most simple of tasks: we drove around and looked for "assets" that no one had noticed before. We were able to connect the dots and uncover what the city could build upon to become a true destination.

Oakland Park didn't have industry clusters or desirable geographic features to draw from. There was no hospital nearby to attract doctors' offices; there wasn't a courthouse to attract law firms and the restaurants and shops that follow office uses; and there wasn't enough raw land to market to anyone for building a new cluster of activity. It was a blue-collar city with a population of about 40,000, with Main Street divided by a railroad, and a large stock of industrial buildings sprinkled throughout. There was no beach, no mountain range views, and no historical venues to capitalize on. And, although the master plan identified public improvements and recommended garage locations for offices, it didn't identify a true vision, so no one came.

For an area to truly become a place where people want to be and businesses want to open, people must feel strongly about the type of environment that will be created when reinvention occurs. People like to be in places where other people are. In its most rudimentary form, human nature is to gather and be around other people. It creates a sense of purpose and safety and is more interesting than sitting alone. A recent Gallup poll noted some key characteristics about what makes people like where they live. These included an attractive physical environment, activity and things to do, and a welcoming feeling or sense of acceptance. These components need to be translated into a clearly defined vision before an area will morph.

In the case of Oakland Park, it seemed to lack any real assets. What it did have, however, was a unique mix of culinary uses within a five-mile radius. In an old warehouse, there was a wholesale kitchen and bath store, nearby there was a large catering firm. On the main commercial boulevard, there was a retail outlet that offered cooking classes. There was only one restaurant with five tables, but it catered to foodies who would pick up unique dishes for their cocktail parties and high-end get-togethers. It became apparent that Oakland Park did have assets, but the planners and consultants brought in to create the master plan didn't consider them in the overall redevelopment process. Nor did they consider the importance of identifying what it was about the area that would make people want to come there. Simply having a master plan with garage locations and sites for future development won't result in redevelopment.

After a careful review of Oakland Park's "assets," limited as they were, along with garnering a deep understanding of what types of businesses could be attracted to the city based on land values, land configurations, street grids, etc., the vision that we ultimately helped Oakland Park create was that of a *Culinary District!*

The City of Oakland Park would ultimately brand its entire downtown around a place that would become a hub for all things culinary! It only took a single presentation of the vision to hit YouTube, and within one week, a brewery called asking if it was feasible to locate an "industrial use" in "downtown." Normally, modern zoning laws would prohibit an industrial use downtown, but suddenly, those vacant, abandoned warehouses became a unique combination of re-use. Then, the warehouses located in and around the downtown suddenly became a HUGE asset! Within eighteen months, an 18,000-square-foot brewery opened, and so began the new brand of downtown Oakland Park. Other businesses were soon interested in joining the concept, including a bakery, an ethnic market, and a health store. A local college even expressed interest in opening a culinary branch. An urban farm was created on vacant land nearby, and suddenly Oakland Park had a vision it could call its own. This is a small example of how simply tweaking a master plan resulted in a new lease on life for a city that had struggled and languished. Not all these businesses will open and some may not even succeed, but once the foundation for a solid brand is established, the city can systematically work on growing it's brand. For many cities looking for a niche to reinvent, the "assets" are most likely already there; you simply need to have the vision to see them, or at a minimum, you need to be willing to think creatively.

Sometimes vision and clarity come to leadership through experiences. Former Mayor Nancy Graham of West Palm Beach said her "Eureka!" moment came when she attended the Mayors' Design Institute in the 1990s. "It really sunk in how important design is," she said. Although she had a vision and ideas on the importance of certain aspects of revitalizing the downtown, a key component to success was found in the design aspects of the redevelopment program. This newly acquired understanding played a major role in her oversight of West Palm Beach's CityPlace project, one of the country's first and largest mixed-use centers at the time. Later Mayor Graham noted that another mayor/redevelopment pro, Joe Riley of Charleston, South Carolina, became her mentor. Mayor Riley had been working on Charleston since 1975, when as a young thirty-two-year-old attorney, he had taken the reins of the fairly blighted downtown and systematically began to change the town's complexion. By the time Mayor Graham encountered Riley, he had a string of successes to his credit, and a fairly strong conviction for the role a vision must play to achieve success.

The Invisible Downtown—Pompano Beach

Sometimes creating the vision for an area isn't the difficult part. Some urban professionals can see through the broken facades and structures, the vacant storefronts and the lack of public investments, and see a thriving entertainment district, for example, complete with cultural uses and new residential buildings.

Bank and Bailey Building. Downtown Pompano Beach, Florida

They see the walkable streets and the urban points of interest. Sometimes, however, city residents, stakeholders and leaders don't see it for years, if ever.

Pompano Beach had an amazing opportunity to re-create its downtown using a historic structure next to an old bank building that had quite a story behind it. The old Bailey Hotel was a two-story building with a grand staircase going straight up through the second floor with a skylight that let light waft in from above. You can see the massive sky-light structure on the roof of the building in the photo on page 5. Surrounding the platform under the skylight, each hotel room had an entry door plus a pane of glass that faced inward on the large center common area. The hotel rooms also had windows facing the streets; there was plenty of natural light in the rooms and grandeur about the place, due to the grand staircase and skylight. The hotel was built in the 1920s, and for a Florida city, that was quite old. Only one other building had the same approximate age and that was the Bank Building.

The following is an excerpt from a book by local historian Dan Hobby describing the events that gave the bank its infamous history:

> *Southeast Florida's contribution to early twentieth-century gangster lore was the Ashley Gang, so-named after its leader, John Ashley. By 1924, the gang had terrorized bankers and mocked lawmen throughout South Florida for over a decade. From their hideouts in the Everglades, they would, at random times, suddenly emerge and pounce on banks and other likely victims. Like other gangsters of the period, they achieved cult status, with many of the "common folk" seeing Ashley as a modern day Robin Hood.*
>
> *At about 2:30 in the afternoon, [Shorty] Lynn, [Clarence] Middleton and [John] Ashley entered the bank simultaneously. C. H. Cates, the cashier, and his assistant were the only persons in the bank, and they were engaged in making up the day's balance. At the sharp command of "Hands Up!" from Lynn, both men looked up and found themselves covered by the three gunmen who were stationed at each*

of the three tellers' windows. Lynn and Middleton were armed with two .45's each, while Ashley had an automatic rifle.

When Cates and his assistant raised their hands, Middleton entered the cage and ordered the bankers out into the lobby, keeping them covered with his pistols. Upon reaching the lobby, they were turned over to Ashley who kept them covered with his rifle while Lynn and Middleton went into the enclosure. Lynn entered the vault and procured $5,000 in cash and $18,000 in securities while Middleton rifled the cash drawers and teller's tray of several thousand dollars. The men worked quickly and without comment, and returned to the lobby in a very few minutes. Looking out the door Lynn signaled and an automobile drove up almost immediately. Tracey was driving the car, and as it stopped in front of the bank Ashley handed Cates a rifle bullet, telling him it was a souvenir of his career as a bank robber.

Driving rapidly through the main street of the town, one of the men waved a bottle of liquor and shouted, "We got it all!"

After abandoning the automobile, the gang crossed the canal in some unknown manner, and their trail was lost in their old haven— the everglades [sic].

The Bank of Pompano fell victim to the Great Depression and went out of business in November 1931. Several years later, William Kester purchased the Bank of Pompano building and opened the Farmers Bank of Pompano. It remained Pompano's only banking institution until the 1950s.

By 2005, both the bank building and the Bailey Hotel had fallen into such disrepair that they were both slated for demolition. A county commissioner begged a local businessman to intervene and purchase the buildings to save them, which he did. He then found himself in the unfortunate position of owning two dilapidated buildings in an area with no vision!

The old downtown where the buildings were located was quite small and compact with only seven other buildings on that main street. The road terminated at a railroad track and turned north with two more small blocks of old and blighted buildings from the '50s and '60s. There was a big, open, dirt lot at the end of the street along the railroad tracks, and the whole downtown area sat on a busy six-lane intersection that was unattractive and pedestrian unfriendly. Most of the retail bays had become storage or wholesale uses, such as pest control supply companies and nothing about the downtown was attractive.

Eventually, city commissioners began to put pressure on the new owners of the bank and hotel buildings to fix up the properties. The owners were afraid to invest huge sums into the properties, knowing no one was interested in renting them, certainly not at the rents needed to cover the rehab expenses.

To compound the situation, the area to the west was an African American community that had been the target of local redevelopment activity for the previous fifteen years. However, the predominant activity had been the acquisition and demolition of properties along the main street, which

Massive roadway system cuts downtown into sections. Pompano Beach, Florida

The Vision 9

Flagler Avenue, before renovation. Pompano Beach, Florida

Flagler Avenue, after renovation. Pompano Beach, Florida

was called MLK Boulevard. The community felt slighted and believed that urban "removal"—not urban "renewal"—was underway.

On the other side of downtown sat City Hall in the middle of ten acres of vacant land. Three areas were divided by six lanes of highway, so not only did the entire area lack vision, it certainly wasn't configured in a typical downtown grid. Forget walking from one part of town to the other.

These conditions sat stagnant for over thirty years, and although there had been attempts to address the blight along MLK Boulevard and in the downtown core, nothing else was being done. There was no vision. As a result, no one came.

One Northwest resident insisted that any plans to renovate the area needed to be focused on the MLK Boulevard only, because that community deserved attention first. Other community members didn't want to see any investment "east of the tracks" where the old bank and hotel sat.

There was no question, however, that the vision should include renovating "Old Town" using the old bank and Bailey Hotel buildings to create a unique and thriving historic district, with restaurants, shops and cultural uses. The Bailey Building would be turned into a cultural hub, using the individual hotel rooms as art hubs. The bank building would be a hot new restaurant.

Across the street the "City Civic Commons" area, where City Hall sat, would include a large cultural building and library on one side and open space for future offices on the other. To the west, the MLK corridor would enjoy activities in another historic building called the "Ali Building," which would focus on the African American library and cultural venue.

The vision almost got bogged down in push-back from folks who were angry that any investment would be realized east of the tracks in the downtown area. The vision didn't get stopped, however, and today the downtown is undergoing the biggest transformation in the city's history.

It is important to keep the vision intact and not allow criticisms of individual components to derail the vision as a whole. In this case, the challenge was that not everyone shared the vision, and understandably, considering how passionately some people felt about a perceived inequity. The issue was compounded because the "Old Town" part of the downtown center would become the main job generator, with restaurants and other job-generating businesses. If Old Town was not allowed to be part of the redevelopment plan, the surrounding areas could not be redeveloped on their own. Before long, the elected officials found themselves stuck between residents of the Northwest community and their angst about any investment east of the tracks, and the redevelopment professionals professing to have the appropriate redevelopment approach.

This scenario plays out all over the United States, and even worldwide, due to cultural and racial biases. These are real issues, and they can be a detriment to changing a city's economic health. They can erode a vision to the point that it can fall apart and must be managed carefully.

The renovated Bailey Hotel, now a successful cultural venue for visual and performing arts. Pompano Beach, Florida

Charrettes, Charrettes, and More Charrettes

Let's say a city has the right vision, but has allowed key components to be removed from the vision, due to pressure from residents or business owners. What if the community has been through years of charrettes, or collaborative sessions, and community forums and produced a "master plan" that lays out their "vision," and everyone, including the residents, the advisory committee members and the elected officials have all endorsed the vision? What happens when they start down the path of implementation, and the newly hired executive implementers (in this case, it was us) brought in to implement the plan tells them it's wrong?!

For any vision to work there must be buy-in. But more importantly, the buy-in needs to be neutral, and the vision can't pander to a select group of individuals who have tried to influence the plan to suit their own needs to the detriment of the whole plan.

A very good example happened in Pompano Beach, Florida. After a two-year process, a master plan was created that included a complete restoration of a dune system, renovated walkways and pathways for residents and tourists, beach pavilions and a surface parking lot that was slated for redevelopment to include limited restaurant and shops. Anchored by its pier, the five-block beachfront area had no other parking. No parking? NO PARKING?! We were hired to manage this city's redevelopment program, so we asked why the city accepted a master plan that excluded any and all parking along the beachfront. We were told the condominium owners didn't want people parking on the street. In fact, the condo owners were proud of the fact they had fought hard to eliminate all parking along the beach years ago. The result was a 60-foot-wide, two-lane speedway! The elected officials, including the district commissioner, said the subject had been beaten to death and revisiting the on-street parking was not an option. The beach redevelopment would continue without parking on the beach.

Obviously, we struggled with how to approach this little dilemma.

There were very vocal community leaders who had led the charge against beachfront parking, and the district commissioner was not about to challenge them. The residents were adamant, and there was no one else in the city paying attention to the issue. To compound matters, at one meeting about 100 residents showed up in red shirts to remind the commissioners that they were united and had no tolerance for any discussion about parking at the beach. We knew, however, that to have a successful beachfront, people needed to be able to park once they got there.

We determined that other voices needed to be heard on the subject, not just the residents of the condos along the beach. Obviously, the condo residents were the ones most affected; however, they did not have the right to drive the City's vision to suit "only their version" of that vision.

We decided to approach other groups in the city to see if they also had concerns about the intent to exclude parking and what they thought of this idea. A series of meetings were held with the local economic development organization, the Chamber of Commerce, the Rotary Club, business owners, the historical club, and any other club that would have us. These groups provided the backbone of our new approach and were very instrumental in changing the future course of the city. Focus groups were held with civic associations to gauge their interest in taking a position on access to beachfront parking. The developers of the pier lot that was slated to become a destination of restaurants and shops began to speak about the need for parking to ensure the new restaurants would survive. Even some restauranteurs got engaged and said they would not invest on the prime beachfront lot if there was not adequate parking. It became clear that the vision was broken by one key element.

Eventually, the discussion circled back to the district commissioner, the advisory committee and the beach residents, all of whom adamantly opposed the parking. To the district commissioner's credit, after numerous meetings and discussions on the subject, he began to see the damage to the overall vision that eliminating the parking would create. He recognized the need to concede that some on-street parking was vital to the success of the future restaurants, and even to provide parking for visitors trying to access the beach. But how could he do a complete turnaround, a 180-degree change,

Lamar Fisher. Mayor, Pompano Beach, Florida

a complete about-face? With dignity and grace, he outlined his original position to the fuming residents, and the crowds threatening to run him out of office. Then, he made his case to the rest of the commission to get their support. With the strong support of the Advisory Chair (the Mayor) who played a key role in keeping control during raucous public meetings, the tides turned (no pun intended). A year later, and this time around, the room was filled with business owners, residents (not in red shirts), property owners, future restaurant owners, and others, all stating the beach was theirs too, and they wanted parking! After a strained silence, the mayor said, "Wow, something has changed in our city." For the first time in twenty years, the stronghold that a few individuals had on the beach was broken and a broken element of the vision was fixed.

The vision plan was revised and one of the most beautiful beach redevelopment projects in Florida was completed in the City of Pompano Beach. The parking revenue went from $300,000 a year to over $2 million a year, enabling the creation of a parking fund to pay for a garage at a nearby vacant lot. The beach project has won numerous awards; but best of all, the very same residents who initially showed up in red shirts, changed their minds and started e-mailing the commission that they were wrong. The beach was beautiful and they were fortunate to be living there. There have been hundreds of e-mails praising the renovations. Oh and by the way, the district commissioner at the center of this controversy got re-elected.

The Vision 15

Original Pompano Beach streetscape plan with no parking

Newly completed beach front parking. Pompano Beach, Florida

2
LEADERSHIP AND POLITICS

Reinventing your city cannot happen without a leader. A leader is required to shape the vision, to make sure the right people are in place to implement the vision, and to navigate the politics that are an ever-constant source of distraction from the vision. Finding the right leader, or recognizing that you already have a leader who can lead the reinvention, is the second step to turning your city around. The key leadership roles that are played in major redevelopment efforts are always obvious AFTER the reinvention has occurred. There is always a person, or a group of people, who can easily be identified as the "leaders" who managed to stay focused and bring about change. Today in Detroit, for example, those leaders may not be readily apparent; their identity as leaders will be revealed in the final description of what ultimately happens to reinvent Detroit. In all cases, however, there must be strong leadership to make the tough and often politically unpopular decisions, or reinvention won't occur.

When we traveled to Bilbao, Spain, we met not one, but several leaders who managed Bilbao's vision. To study the transformation of that Basque city, we interviewed many people who had been involved in the transformation over the past twenty years, including city staffers, the mayor, the executive teams, major organizations, university representatives and others. One of our most enlightening interviews was with Alfonso Martinez Cearra, director of Metropoli-30, the entity that guided the vision. The name Metropoli-30 was created when the transformation started, and was meant to convey the image of what the metropolis would look like after thirty years. Bilbao managed to go from a severely blighted industrial city (think any steel town, USA) to a thriving metropolis in twenty-five years! We have watched small cities that only manage to redo a few streetscapes in twenty five years, let alone get billions of dollars invested in transportation, renew an entire river system and attract the interest of the Guggenheim Museum!

Both Alfonso and Mayor Ibon Areso told funny, yet poignant, stories about how the famous Guggenheim Museum came to Bilbao. After all, the choices were between Bilbao, a little-known Spanish enclave with no real assets, or Salzburg, Austria, a thriving and historic, culturally driven city. According to Alfonso, Bilbao said the magic words, "I love you," meaning "we love who you are, Guggenheim Museum, and what you represent, and we want you more than anything in the world." Salzburg leaders apparently told the Guggenheim something like, "Yeah, come if you want." Salzburg already had such a culturally rich city, they didn't covet a massive museum. Mayor Areso framed it another way: "Either the Guggenheim could go back to the United States as a bachelor, or marry the ugly bride—Bilbao." Obviously, the Guggenheim chose Bilbao, and it turned out to be a Cinderella story. The museum made Bilbao citizens so proud after feeling "ugly" for decades—it renewed their faith in their city and in its future.

The leaders in Bilbao knew their strengths, and their weaknesses. They knew that to change they had to make major commitments. It's how they did it that is so informative. After all, Alfonso said, "the Basques are not humble people, but we knew we had to court the museum and show our desire."

Alfonso was adamant that what drove the leaders at the time wasn't so much a crisis, but fear; fear and uncertainty of how everyone would survive. Alfonso explained that the area was so blighted many had lost hope; unemployment was raging and no new buildings or housing had been built for decades. In fact, the river was so polluted, he said, "It wasn't a question of how sick you will get when you fall in the river. It's will you live if you fall in the river? Where there is uncertainty, there must be leadership. And their main role is to point in a direction."

Alfonso also opined, "If there is no leadership, there will be anti-leadership."

In the 1960's, a leadership vacuum in The Hague, Netherlands, caused the central business district to fall victim to debilitating suburban designs on downtown roads. Residents were moving to the suburbs and large roadways were built downtown detracting from an urban pedestrian environment. The government had placed a strong emphasis on public housing and paid little attention to attracting private investment. Eventually, a strong pushback from the public resulted in one of the leaders, Adri Duivesteijn, to challenge the construction of massive road projects. He focused on investing in public improvements that would attract private investment, not just huge road projects. Duivesteijn, as The Hague's committed leader, set the stage for decades of sound transportation policies that in turn attracted new development. In 2015, The Hague was awarded the titled "Best City Center in the Netherlands."

How many times have we seen a city which lacks a strong leader become a place for negativity and small-mindedness to exist. The people who want to criticize and place blame on everything and everyone thrive in these environments. A true leader can't let that happen. Granted, they have the challenge of listening to the public, but they cannot let a small minority of the public hijack the city and put it into a catatonic state. The mayor or civic leaders can't let these types of anti-leaders get a stronghold at a meeting, interrogate staff from the microphone, or threaten and insult employees or fellow commissioners. They can't let them derail community forums, or take over as "visionaries." If they do, the anti-leaders will appear strong and in charge. We're not saying all leaders and their plans are so bullet-proof and perfect that the community should stay silent and follow like sheep. We're saying that for progress to happen, leaders need to be in key positions to convey the vision, keep everyone focused, and avoid the fits and starts that can plague a reinvention process.

Obviously, effective leadership by elected officials is a must for any reinvention initiative to succeed. And conversely, if the elected officials are not engaged in the process, or do not believe that reinvention should occur, chances are the efforts are dead in the water. So, let's assume that at some point in time, there is enough momentum from within the community that it has defined a problem that needs to be fixed, and that redevelopment of an area is a priority. The streets have potholes and no vision (Vancouver 1980), there is high crime and a high vacancy rate downtown (Charleston 1975), there's not enough investment occurring (Fort Lauderdale 1975), the town is in shambles (Detroit 2009), or the area was once a great place, but has changed and no longer has its same allure (Times Square 1985).

One of the most visionary and complicated reinvention projects happened on the small island of Aruba in the Caribbean. Its leader was Eduardo de Veer, a successful businessman who ran various companies on the small island, including the Coca-Cola bottling plant and the port operation for cargo. With a small population, and a land mass that was only twenty miles long, tourism was the number one industry—the only industry, really. He knew there was opportunity to promote the quaint downtown, but the island only had one major roadway connecting various parts of the island, and that one roadway cut between the downtown and the ocean. There was virtually no allure, other than the beaches. Some people poked fun at the island's attempt to create beautiful architectural facades, but those were fake copies of the real thing in neighboring Curacao. Aruba, formerly a Dutch territory, was a favorite stomping ground for American tourists, because they liked the seven-mile stretch of white, sandy beaches with American hotel chains, which provided a safe and familiar experience in a foreign country. All the locals spoke English, and unless you were looking for adventure travel or something more historic, Aruba was the perfect spot for sun and sea.

De Veer determined that the downtown needed to compete with neighboring Curacao, a truly historical downtown with buildings that were 300 years old. And Aruba needed something to redefine the downtown, including a hotel. The problem was that the main drag that connected one

Leadership and Politics 21

Renaissance Aruba Resort & Casino. Hotel guest boat launch inside the hotel.

Renaissance Aruba Resort & Casino. Boat entrance channel under roadway.

end of the island to the other ran alongside the perimeter of downtown, cutting off beachfront access for a hotel. There was no beach, just a rocky shore. De Veer contemplated moving the street, but that wouldn't solve the problem because there still wasn't a beach across the street that could be utilized. How could he operate a downtown hotel on the water with no beach access? And how could he compete with all the other hotels that sat on that gorgeous seven-mile stretch of white sand?

De Veer envisioned that the only way to have a hotel downtown was to bring the ocean to the hotel. He bought a nearby island and dug a canal under the main roadway system. Once the canal was completed, boats would come under the street right into the lobby of his hotel and shuttle guests to and from his island's "private beach!" Aside from the obvious engineering issues that idea posed, there was a political hill to climb and multiple people to convince. Clearly, De Veer's vision took leadership.

Maintaining the Vision

Mayor Nancy Graham. West Palm Beach, Florida, 1991–1999

Our objective in stressing the significance of leadership is not to analyze the political success of any individual elected official; rather, it is to emphasize the impact a leader has on the vision. Whether it is a long-serving single leader or a succession of leaders, the key is maintaining the vision.

One of the largest and most successful public/private, mixed-use redevelopment projects in the country is the CityPlace project in West Palm Beach, Florida. The story of CityPlace is fascinating and has many elements that made the project what it is today. It started

Leadership and Politics   **23**

Mayor/Congresswoman Lois Frankel. West Palm Beach, Florida, 2003–2011

Mayor Jeri Muoio, Ph.D. West Palm Beach, Florida, 2011–

with leadership. Had there not been an aggressive leader championing the redevelopment and going against the critics who were predicting a massive failure, the project would have crumbled under the weight of the naysayers. The project was also high-risk for the developers because there wasn't a comparable project to point to elsewhere in the south Florida area. Lenders were not going to line up to fund a risky project, so the partnership between the city and the developer was key.

So, what role did leadership play in CityPlace? Actually the story is still being written. Even so, we can begin with the original mayor, Nancy Graham, who can clearly be credited with visioning and starting the implementation of the project along with her team in the 1990s. Once CityPlace was built, two future mayors, Joel Daves and Lois Frankel, who later went on to become Congresswoman Frankel, led the continued development of the surrounding parcels, resulting in the next phase of the project, including a commercial tower that sold for top dollar once it was complete. The fourth mayor,

Jeri Muoio, was at the helm when one of the most important final elements of the 72-acre project came to fruition—the Palm Beach County Convention Center Hotel. Over a span of more than twenty years (1990's–2010's), these mayors played key roles in providing leadership for the CityPlace project and enabled it to continue its evolution into one of the most important projects that has defined downtown West Palm Beach.

CityPlace Beginnings

In the mid-1990s, a group of private developers targeted a blighted African American neighborhood on the southern fringe of downtown West Palm Beach for redevelopment. Vacant houses throughout the area were being used for prostitution and selling drugs. A bold plan called for acquisition of over 72 acres of land, and redevelopment of the area as a large-scale, mixed-use project.

After several years of painfully slow acquisition and demolition of over 100 single family homes, the original developers ran out of money. Bankruptcy followed, during the economic downturn of the late '90s. Acres of vacant land marred a gateway entrance to the city and no developer could take a chance on picking up where the original developers stopped because title to the 72 acres was so fractured.

In 1991, Nancy Graham, a practicing land use and environmental lawyer, was elected the city's first "strong mayor." Even though the city had created a redevelopment agency in 1984 that could direct and fund redevelopment, efforts were largely diluted and there really wasn't any bang for the buck. The combination of a strong mayor and all the authority that came with it, backed by the powerful redevelopment agency as a tool, proved to be the magic potion that enabled Graham (a strong visionary and leader) to begin meaningful redevelopment. And that she did. She started with a plan for the downtown and followed that reinvention with what we know today as "CityPlace."

Graham told us that when she became mayor, she knew she needed short and long-term visions. She needed something to happen right away, and thought there was a need to show progress fairly quickly. She began assembling a team to plan and implement her ideas.

She used her in-house team and outside consultants to more clearly define the vision, and in 1993, she used the mayor's spending authority (up to $50,000) to buy a blighted hotel in the heart of downtown at a foreclosure sale. She created interest and enthusiasm for her vision by imploding the old hotel at midnight on New Year's Eve. Graham's plan for that area of the downtown featured fountains and an amphitheater, and other public improvements that would polish up the city's dull and tired image, just in time for the its centennial celebration in 1994. She then put together a plan with the financial folks and the DDA, and headed to New York to convince the rating agency, Moody's, that she could get the city back on track with the new plan. "I bet over a steak dinner that the vision would change the city's rating, and it did" she said. The bond amount was $15 million, and by early 1994, construction of the plan was underway. Like many strong leaders, she showed conviction in her actions, but lamented her position at the time, stating, "Look, we don't have anywhere to go but up. We can't sit on our thumbs and do nothing!"

As with many redevelopment initiatives, lots of people didn't want the change she was promoting. The city needed somebody strong enough to forge ahead, despite a few vocal, local critics who didn't want any form of change. But, the city also needed a leader who would listen and build a good solid project that could be successful.

While the downtown plan was unfolding, the vision for the redevelopment of the 72-acre site was starting to gain traction. Ten acres had already been donated, and the Kravis Center for the Performing Arts had been built. All of the parcels had been demolished (except for the historic former 1920's Methodist church), so Graham met with developers, owners, etc., to try to get the project reinvigorated. Because of the fractured title, the city was the only entity with the power of eminent domain (which power has subsequently been diminished in the area of redevelopment) which could, in turn, give it the ability to clear title to all the parcels. "It was so bogged down with foreclosures; the previous developer had failed and slowly sold his development rights off, making it extremely difficult to assemble. I worked with the city attorney and the city manager quietly to put together a strategy to buy the property. We put together a budget and negotiated out most of the land for the deal, and went to court on the two remaining parcels. We came within $100,000 of budget to acquire the property." The focused commitment to redevelopment of the site required a great deal of leadership from the mayor and the city commission. Today, many do not realize how many times the project could have been derailed, but for their unwavering commitment!

Graham knew that, as the leader, she would need to deal with some of the more difficult property owners who were looking to capitalize on the city's plan only to benefit themselves, even at the risk of messing up the entire redevelopment. Property owners wanted more money for their property than it was worth, and I said, "Look, property owner, you need to work with us." Most eventually came around after hard negotiations.

Graham also noted, "Most cities don't have enough people on staff to negotiate sophisticated real estate deals, so we brought in attorneys and hired inside and outside counsel and consultants. We caught flak for not always using locals." One of our favorite quotes from Graham is: "Redevelopment is not for the weak at heart."

Ultimately, a bid was issued for redevelopment of the 72-acre parcel. Three proposals were submitted, and New York-based Related Group was chosen over a local firm. The Related Group is led by Ken Himmel and is owned by Steve Ross of the Related Companies (currently the owner of the Miami Dolphins), the Related Group of Florida/Jorge Perez, and the O'Conner Group of New York.

Howard Elkus, Related's architect, created the vision of a grand, Italian-style town with a central plaza, appropriately scaled streets, walkable sidewalks, fountains and focal points of interest. Parking would be concealed and "disappear" into the folds of the project so as to not distract from the authentic feel of the area. The mayor and members of the team even traveled to Italy, seeking true world examples that would ensure the size and scale of the project represented old-world charm.

Shortly after the Italy trip, a big glitch occurred because the plan called for razing the former 1920's historic Methodist church. The outcry over demolishing the structure was so widespread, Graham decided that somehow the architect would have to incorporate the church building into the overall project. It was restored to its original form and turned into a theatre and event venue. Graham's decision illustrates that leadership wasn't about winning a battle over the church's demolition, it was about ensuring that the building fits with the overall vision and that it could be physically incorporated into the project. Graham found the perfect compromise for both the public and the private sectors she represented. Had Graham pushed for demolition of the church, she might have won that battle, and lost the war What is known today as the Harriet Himmel Gilman Theater has become one of the most beloved and successful aspects of the CityPlace project. To this day, tours are given by talented local architect Rick Gonzalez showing how the church was restored to its original grandeur and was seamlessly incorporated into the overall CityPlace design. Today, it's used for civic events, private gatherings, and art and cultural forums. It is a true historical treasure of the city that actually validated the goal of creating "old world" charm in a new city. Gonzalez' design and restoration of the old church

Seventy-two acre assemblage with Harriet Himmel Gilman Theater (center). West Palm Beach, Florida

into a vibrant mixed-use building has been called the heart and soul of CityPlace by the Urban Land Institute.

The CityPlace project called for a mixed-use development with retail on the ground floor and residential overhead, a grand plaza area with a euro-style central fountain, parking garages, a convention center hotel, a 350,000-square-foot commercial office tower, and additional future office space on outparcels. The initial phase of the retail and residential project opened in 2000. The project was extremely complex and required a development agreement between the city, the community redevelopment agency (CRA) and the developers to define who would pay for what. The CRA issued a $50 million bond to build the public portions of the project, namely the garages, streets, sidewalks and plazas. The repayment source for the bond debt was the new taxes that were generated as a result of the project. This funding source is commonly referred to as tax increment financing (TIF) and is a valuable tool for large-scale redevelopment projects. In the end, a $250 million project was built, and at the time of this writing, the project has generated enough tax increment to pay off the public investment in the garage and street improvements!

After two terms, Graham left office in 1999. Joel Daves succeeded Graham as mayor and pushed for more downtown housing during his single term. Then, Lois Frankel was elected mayor in 2003 and, like Graham, served for two terms.

CityPlace was successful, but continued leadership was necessary to ensure the entire downtown would thrive. "I can hearken you back to the conditions when I became mayor," Frankel told us. "The whole eastern downtown had deteriorated due to traffic, road construction and the newness of CityPlace." A large sucking sound was almost audible as shops and anchor tenants left Clematis, the city's main street, and relocated to CityPlace. It was like they got caught in a vacuum and emptied almost overnight to the sparkling new project. Over time, "the only businesses that had success (in the main street area) were bars at night, so we had a huge crime problem. It was horrible," Frankel said.

Leadership and Politics 29

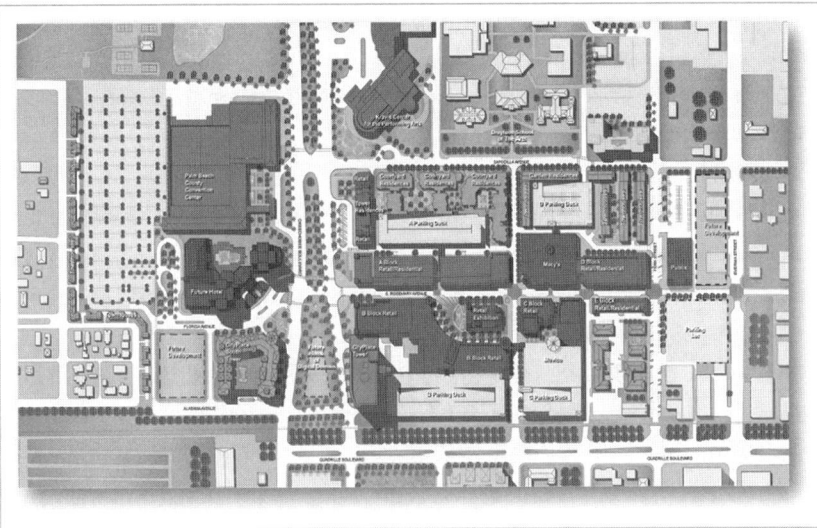

CityPlace site map. West Palm Beach, Florida

Harriet Himmel Gilman Theater at CityPlace. West Palm Beach, Florida

Similarly, in the north end of town—an area called Northwood—there wasn't even a glimpse of hope. Drugs and prostitution, and their related criminal activities, were prevalent, so even though the area had potential and good bones, it was failing.

Much progress had been made in the city; some of the successes, however, created new problems, which is often a less desirable effect of redevelopment initiatives. The main street became a ghost town, and the remaining merchants were crying foul, because the city was a partner in CityPlace. One of the options to improve the downtown was to do a joint streetscape project with the State of Florida and upgrade the roadways with improved sidewalks, new pedestrian lighting and on-street parking. The road construction only compounded the pain the downtown retailers were feeling and more merchants went out of business. The state project was delayed and was often called one of the worst-managed public projects in the state's history. At one point, Mayor Frankel got so fed up with the calls and criticism from the merchants and residents, she installed flashing message boards along the entire grid of the street project, and posted the governor's phone number, instructing people to call him. It was a state project after all. With the heat now on the governor, suddenly the streetscape project started to move and was completed without further delay. Not only did Mayor Frankel demonstrate intolerance to shoddy construction, she took a strong leadership position, even if it meant aggravating the governor. Frankel was an extremely effective leader who had the ability to listen and understand both sides of any debate, and then proceed based on a clear vision with a defined end result.

Frankel had no local government experience when she became mayor, but she had spent time as a state representative in Tallahassee, the state's capital. Her eyes were first opened to the real possibilities within the downtown when she attended the annual boat show. "What I couldn't believe was how many people were coming down to the waterfront," she said. She immediately recognized the appeal of the city's waterfront and shortly afterward invited the Urban Land Institute (ULI) to bring a panel to West Palm Beach. ULI studied the downtown and determined that, if the main street could be extended to the waterway, it would revitalize. That meant demolishing the existing library, which didn't go over very well with some residents. It also meant purchasing a city block in the middle of the downtown that housed a long-vacant department store-sized building so the library and city hall could be relocated. As the leader, Frankel felt there were some leadership traits that were important to the success of the project, including building consensus to weather the storm of opposition that always comes with initiating large redevelopment projects. "Many people wanted to see the downtown plan implemented, but many did not, so you have to build consensus" she said. "You will need it." Frankel recognized that she needed to be open to new ideas and unafraid to make hard decisions. "You have to be open and flexible, but in terms of leadership, an important rule is, don't be afraid to make decisions. Don't keep waiting or changing course because there may be a better way to do it tomorrow. Especially in leadership, there's no perfect solution."

Once the Clematis streetscape was complete, Mayor Frankel tasked the Downtown Development Authority (DDA) with attracting new tenants and filling the vacancies created by the CityPlace vacuum that consumed many of the main street retailers. She recognized that, although CityPlace was a successful addition to the downtown, there needed to be more elements for a great downtown. Frankel instructed her staff to determine the bonding capacity of the CRA, and ultimately issued a $100 million bond to make further investments in the downtown. Those investments would incorporate the plan created by the Urban Land Institute. The projects would include a major redesign of the city's waterfront, construction of a new City Hall, a state-of-the-art library, with space for cultural uses, and new parking structures. Like Graham, Frankel took a team on a road trip to analyze the best examples of libraries, city halls and waterfronts. Also like Graham, she was bombarded with criticism, but forged ahead anyway. City Center, the reinvented hub for city government boasts a lively central plaza and a public library that draws over a million visitors a year. Within the library, there is space for a private vendor, occupied today by Dunkin Donuts. This major

Nancy Graham Fountain on Clematis Street. West Palm Beach, Florida

project, located in the middle of Clematis Street brought new life to the street, new vendors and an entirely new energy. The newly designed waterfront produced an unparalleled location for the city's green market, the Lake Pavilion, a highly successful public event and private occasion venue that has floor to ceiling views of the Intracoastal Waterway, and the "Great Lawn," a vast open green space graced with curving pathways, soothing water features and a perfect location for "Movies on the Green," concerts and other large-scale public events.

The results took years to produce, but the continued investment has taken the city to the next level and put it in the spotlight nationally.

With the $100 million bond issued and many of the projects the funds were earmarked for completed, a new era for West Palm Beach began in March, 2011, when Jeri Muoio was elected mayor.

By 2011, an announcement was made about locating an outlet mall with over one million square feet of space at an abandoned mall site a few miles away. Now it was CityPlace's turn to fear the vacuum effect. The CityPlace developers feared CityPlace would meet the same fate it had imposed on Clematis Street downtown, and that shoppers would abandon the downtown retailers in place of the new shopping outlet center. The Related

Companies approached the CRA and began to devise plans for remerchandising CityPlace so they could stay ahead of the impending shift of retail activity in the city. About the same time, Related had won the award to build the Convention Center Hotel and was trying to arrange another public/private deal to help finance the project. Unlike the CityPlace project, the county was involved in the hotel deal, and it took leadership from the governing bodies to craft an agreement that involved subsidies from both the city and the county. The Convention Center Hotel would be yet another key piece in the reinvention of downtown West Palm Beach.

Mayor Muoio had been in leadership positions in the past, including high ranking posts in the education field. Her leadership strategy included "being a collaborative thinker, rather than noodling it alone," she said. "It's easier to dictate, but you need the collaborative approach to see projects to the finish line."

Muoio initially concentrated her attention inward to City Hall operations itself. This approach was sorely needed, because some of the city departments had gotten the reputation of being unfriendly, including the building department, so she focused on changing the perception that it was hard to do projects in West Palm Beach.

Just a side note in defense of building departments who are often painted as the bad guys in the building world: most building departments have dedicated and friendly professionals all working toward the common goal of creating a successful city. Sometimes, however, these officials get overzealous in their mission and invoke their power, rather than consider other available options. Yes, their mission is to uphold the safety standards they are sworn to, and, yes, oftentimes developers want the world, and whine whenever they have to jump through hoops to get their permits and meet the building department demands. But the real issue often isn't about the technical side of a building department; it's about the presence or lack of a can-do, let's-get-it-done attitude. Planning and zoning departments can suffer the same ills and it is extremely important that the city manager, mayor or other strong leader fix this situation as soon as it becomes a problem. If there are continuous complaints about doing business in any city, something is wrong inside city hall and it MUST change. The thought that it's those greedy developers who just want to have their way is a very dangerous position for managers and elected officials to take. If the warning signs go unaddressed, development will go elsewhere and you likely won't even realize it.

This is a test: has any city manager or elected official heard more than three times in a relatively short period of time, that folks have had a terrible time dealing with the same city department? If you answered yes, we guarantee the department is in trouble. If you are not fixing it, watch what will happen over time. For every complaint you hear, there are many more you don't hear about. Then, there are those contractors and developers who wouldn't dare to say anything for fear of retribution. Don't confuse this situation with requiring builders to meet good design standards and follow a lot of rules; those are normal complaints. This is about the situation where people interacting with a city department have had a really bad experience. Strive for what happened in West Palm Beach when Mayor Muoio fixed the problem: incredibly positive change and growth; improved morale with other departments; increased tax base etc.

One city manager we worked with had coffee cups printed with the word NO on it. The NO was surrounded by a circle with a slash through it, meaning saying NO to people doing business with the city was not an option! It didn't mean they had to allow every request, but they had to find a way to help the public through the process without simply saying NO. That was the message he insisted the city department heads convey when doing business with the public, especially in the zoning and building department.

Mayor Muoio knew that employee attitude was at the root of the problem she was facing, and she didn't stop until she found the right solution. The new people she hired to run the department still upheld the letter of the law of the building and zoning codes, still made sure buildings were safe, and still had to say "sort of no" sometimes, because the alternatives were just not buildable. What Muoio's new team really said was, "We will follow the rules and help you get a permit for a safe structure, and we will assist you in finding ways to do that as quickly and efficiently as possible." That change alone transformed the reputation of West Palm Beach into being a welcoming and more business friendly.

One of Muoio's strengths was the ability to build a solid team that shared the same vision. She really got tested when she decided to outsource the redevelopment department. Critics from every nook and cranny came out to oppose her decision. She steadfastly maintained her conviction that, like the building department, the redevelopment department was broken and needed fixing, and she didn't want a conventional fix. Like Graham and Frankel, who took blows for unpopular positions, she stood firm and forged ahead.

She got community input, the city commissioners weighed in, albeit under pressure, and she sought support from key people. "It was a very difficult time; even the Chamber of Commerce didn't want me to privatize! There were a few Chamber members, however, who said this is the kind of thinking we should support. I approached them by saying, 'I've made good decisions in the past.' It took compromise, but we did it."

Her team and her new organization structure are paving the way for the next round of growth for the city. The decision to privatize led to our company's selection to manage the CRA. There is still work to be done on the waterfront, and in other parts of the city, but the succession of aggressive, proactive and strong leaders forged a path for future leaders to follow and build upon.

During our many years of working in community redevelopment, we have interviewed numerous city leaders. Those interviews reveal traits these leaders have in common: they reject status quo; they are studious; they are persistent; and, most importantly, they stay focused on the vision.

3
THE TEAM

Once the vision is clear and the leader is in place, the third step to reinventing your city is assembling the right team. As we saw in the previous chapter, it is a leader, or a set of leaders, who initiate the vision, but the leader cannot do it alone. A team is required to ensure that all areas of expertise needed to carry out the vision are also in place. The team may be selected by the leader; alternatively, the leader may select an executive implementer to assemble the team.

Mayor Inaki Azkuna. Bilbao, Spain

Mayor Ibon Areso. Bilbao, Spain

For example, in West Palm Beach, Nancy Graham, selected and led the team herself. In contrast, almost ten years later, Lois Frankel selected an executive implementer who assembled and led the team. In Charleston, the leader and the executive implementer were one and the same—Mayor Joe Riley. In Bilbao, Spain, the leaders were from various levels of government, including the city, the provincial government, the regional government, and even the central Spanish government. But the city's then mayor, Inaki Azkuna, became the prime leader, and the executive implementer was then Deputy Mayor Ibon Areso. In case after case of successful city-reinvention, the making of a team is essential. It is the team that will initiate and implement the plan.

Role of the Leader

In deciding who to include on the team, a leader must first ask, "What kind of team? What are their qualifications? What is their experience? And what do they do first?" A leader without a redevelopment team to implement

World Symphony. Miami Beach, Florida

the vision to make significant changes to a city starts out like an orchestra conductor without music and musicians. The orchestra conductor must select the musicians who are capable of making beautiful music together.

Start with a Core Team

Start with a small core team. Start with the most highly qualified people you can afford, and select those who can independently direct their discipline, such as finance, rules and regulations (zoning), construction, urban design, marketing, public-private partnership (economic development), engineering (streetscaping and infrastructure), project management, and administration. Start with a core team of no more than three-to-five team members, but select them based upon their ability to convert the vision into a plan. The core team needed to reinvent a city must consist of the following essential disciplines: marketing, urban design, finance, project management and legal.

Marketing Team Member

The marketing team member's task is to brand and promote the city. The brand must relate to the vision. Delray Beach branded its downtown as an "Arts and Entertainment District." It worked. Bilbao branded its city as a world cultural destination and promoted an economy based upon knowledge and technology. The cultural destination worked in Bilbao, and the knowledge and technology brand is developing. Charleston branded its city as an historical tourist destination. Charleston later added a "food" brand to the city as a string of highly successful restaurants opened to meet the demand from visitors. The vision may be very general, or it may be very specific, but the marketing team member must take the vision and wrap a brand around it. Every city must stand for something, or it will be of no interest to residents, visitors, retailers, consumers, and businesses. A city's brand must be easy to understand and catch your attention. Building an indoor football stadium does not brand a city. The marketing team member must translate the early vision into a concrete concept, such as the way Oakland Park, did when it branded its small downtown as a culinary arts district. The comprehensive nature of the culinary arts brand in Oakland Park is being translated into logos, advertising, web site design, business recruitment, incentive programs, and culinary events. Its early success attracted a brewery, bakery, urban farm, major kitchen and bath showroom, kitchen designers and contractors, and restaurants.

The other members of the core team must also join with the marketing team member and be involved, because the brand will have an influence on the work of the other team members' disciplines. For example, the urban designer must understand the brand and contribute to the brand concept as he or she draws a concept of the vision's physical plan. A place, such as a plaza, must be planned so that culinary events and green markets may take place every week to celebrate the brand. In fact, Oakland Park built a plaza at one end of its downtown main street that served to attract customers to eat outdoors and drink beer at the new brewery, procured as a result of the culinary arts district brand.

Urban Design Team Member

The urban designer is a thinker and a visionary. The urban designer must take the initial vision and translate it into a physical plan. The physical plan is part of the overall bigger plan. The plan must have a schedule of public improvements and costs. The plan must be coordinated with the finance team member. And most managers, including the leader, and businesses and the public, will then respond to physical plans and pictures. One of the great planners in America city-making was Major Pierre Charles L'Enfant, who in 1791, after being appointed by the leader, President George Washington, made a city plan for Washington, D.C., a plan which has remained influential for over 200 years.

Bilbao's first plan was not a physical plan, only a policy document. It specifically stated that the plan should be to rebuild its port at a new, more convenient location near the mouth of the river and the bay, to make the industrial river a place for public benefit, featuring a linear park, a recreational facility, and a light rail transportation system. The first plan would make Bilbao a cultural center and a center for knowledge-based, high-tech businesses. Later, Bilbao, after a design competition, hired architect Cesar Pelli to draw up an urban design plan for the first phase of Bilbao's downtown redevelopment. The plan was modified several times after actual businesses and developers were solicited to build their structures. In the end, the Pelli urban design plan effectively set the stage for the types of buildings to be constructed: mid-rise and high-rise office and mixed-use buildings, together with other physical amenities.

Finance Team Member

The finance team member is important to the success of implementation because this member must envision very early the source of the funds to pay for the public improvements, incentives, advertising, land acquisition, parking, transportation systems, and other soft and hard costs of the plan. Bilbao realized that it had hundreds of acres of riverfront owned by the Port Authority, and two Transportation (rail) Authorities that could assist in financing the redevelopment of the downtown with the increase in the value of the public property. The financial team member in Bilbao also knew that a combination of government partners, including the city, the Biskaia Provincial Government, the Autonomous Pais Vasco Government, and the Spanish Central Government, must play a role in funding the billions of euros needed to rebuild Bilbao. It is estimated that Bilbao received over 10 billion euros of public funding to revitalize the city. The financial plan prepared by the financial team member is an essential part of the business plan for the reinvention of a city, and preparation of the financial plan early in the process requires a financial team member with considerable talent.

Project Manager Team Member

The project manager team member is part of the core because this position is in charge of actually building projects, such as new urban streets, transportation systems, utilities infrastructure, parks, river walks, beach fronts, cultural facilities, new governmental facilities, bridges, signage and much more. In fact, once a city is in the rebuilding process, there will be a need for many project managers. The executive implementer must hire as many project managers as necessary to fulfill the plan. These are the positions of the doers and they are essential to getting projects built. The doers may be people from a wide range of backgrounds, such as planning, engineering, construction, architecture, marketing and business. In the Delray Beach story, after the city issued $21.5 in general obligation bonds, it took almost ten years to spend the funds because they did not hire a sufficient number of project managers. Hire as many as necessary to complete projects; it will only speed up the implementation. Project managers must be considered a cost of the project, and with good ones, the managers will pay for themselves.

Legal Team Member

The legal team member is important because there are federal, state and local regulations that need to be followed. Normally, the choice is to defer to the city attorney as the legal team member. This is usually a bad idea for the same reason you don't ask the city manager to be the executive implementer. The city attorney has more work than he or she can handle to solve city issues, including law suits, legal interpretations, zoning conflicts, the normal everyday business of ordinances and resolutions, and many others. Retain an expert outside counsel to handle the substantial task of being a vital member of a long term implementation job. Delray Beach successfully used an outside attorney who managed the legal process and made the tasks of redevelopment much less complicated, and who actively participated in changing some statutory laws to assist redevelopment. There are, of course, exceptions. The City of West Palm Beach used two successive city attorneys with community redevelopment experience to handle the complex legal issues presented by the city's plan.

Isolate the Team from Bureaucracy

If you want to reinvent your city, you must isolate the core team physically and psychologically (but not politically) from government bureaucracy. The leader, such as a mayor, has the job of moving the brand, the plan and the implementation of projects through the political process. In some cases, it may be a very adept executive implementer who moves progress forward. The leader, the executive implementer and the team will have foes, including other bureaucrats, other politicians, and citizens who do not want change. How many times have you heard the comment from one of these groups, "We tried that in the past, but it did not work," or "You can never get that passed by city council," or "The neighborhood will never accept that idea"? Never let your core team be integrated with the enemy. The enemy is the attitude that change cannot be done or that change cannot accomplish anything. In 1942, President Franklin D. Roosevelt sent his Manhattan Project team to Los Alamos in the New Mexican desert to isolate the team from Washington bureaucracy and politics. Don't let the naysayers influence the team members. As an executive implementer working to inspire his team, Chris stopped his subscription to the local newspaper in order to avoid the daily barrage of criticism about redevelopment. Similarly, he started each day with a pep talk about avoiding negative influences. It is also inspiring if the leader comes by from time to time to encourage the team. *Bureaucrats run cities, but **great** leaders reinvent **great** cities.*

Build Your Own Team, Not Someone Else's

As the core team members are selected, there will be many political activists on the sidelines who will try to influence the team composition. A word of advice to the leader and the executive implementer: build your own team, and not someone else's. When the strong mayors were elected in West Palm Beach, they each selected their own team, letting many department heads of the city move onto other opportunities, and adding new team members. During their early days as mayors, people on the sidelines made suggestions to the mayors about appropriate team members. Listen, but always build your own team. Transfer those who don't support the vision, and hire those you want for the team. The leader must be the one with the vision, and each team member must fit harmoniously with the leader's intent. Never hire a team member who is neither loyal nor competent. Never include a team member who does not endorse the vision. Do not hesitate to remove a team member who has become toxic to the team.

Streamline the Reporting Process

In successful city-building, ask how many people and levels of government does an executive implementer or project manager have to go through to get something done? Reinvent government at the outset by having the executive implementer report directly to the leader or the leader's board of directors (city council).

Never have the executive implementer report to a career bureaucrat. Remember the city manager runs the city, but rarely reinvents it. He doesn't have time and that's not the role of a city manager. There are exceptions, however; when the city manager becomes a partner with the executive implementer in executing the vision, that team is unbeatable! If the leader has a board, or is part of the board such as a city council, then the leader must be responsible to that level of approval. If the project manager has to interface with planning, zoning, building, fire, advisory boards, and more, the leader must let the governmental departments know that the redevelopment projects are a priority and they are not to be impeded. The leader must tell the city manager and his department heads, "This is the mission. Make it happen. Let it happen."

Assemble the Full Team after the First Plan

Assembling a team is the work of the executive implementer, and it is never complete. Team members will come and go as the plan evolves, changes and matures. First comes the core team which makes the plan, and then comes the full implementation team, whose job it is to get projects built. The full team consists of the same core team members described earlier, together with others who are added as implementation progresses. The additional disciplines needed to supplement the core team include: an engineer to oversee professional consultants who will design and build new infrastructure; an events manager to attract the public to the newly branded area; a marketing manager who will coordinate the publicity and good will of the implementation; an economic development public/private partnership manager to attract private sector development; a construction project manager overseeing all publically funded construction work; special incentive project managers to assist the small public/private partnerships such as refurbishing existing commercial space; a tenant recruitment manager to recruit commercial tenants to the newly branded city; and administrative personnel, such as someone to keep the records and files well organized. The public is one day going to ask to see the files.

Consultants as Part of the Team

An important complement to the executive implementer's full team is the expert consultant. Although the marketing team member may be in charge of branding the city, or even a project within a city, a marketing consultant may be needed to assist with design and graphics. Other professionals will be needed for other disciplines. Bilbao contracted with an international management consulting firm in New York to recommend a concept or vision for the redevelopment of the city. The document was completed in the late 1980s and adopted in 1991. It was called the *Strategic Plan for the Revitalization of Metropolitan Bilbao* and suggested that Bilbao become a great center of culture. The recommendation received mixed reviews from its citizens, who mainly came from a Basque heritage that had never embodied a culture of the arts. In fact, it was foreign to the Basques in the beginning. Today, Bilbao is a significant center of culture for Spain, and its museums, particularly the Guggenheim, attract over one million visitors a year. Bilbao did not stop at one museum, but, in 2001, also renovated extensively its original Museum of Fine Arts, including its contemporary wing adjacent to its neo-eighteenth century facility. While the Guggenheim attracts visitors from all parts of the world, the Museum of Fine Arts serves as a local social center for the residents and visitors of the city. Visit the museum on a Friday or Saturday night and you will find hundreds of young families walking inside and outside the museum hand-in-hand. The new generation of Basque families in Bilbao has found culture and has adopted it. The Pais Vasco, famous for its fish, farming

Guggenheim Museum. Bilbao, Spain

and sheep cheeses, is now also famous for its culture and its eight Michelin-starred restaurants.

Architecture

A visit to any of the cities we have described will graphically demonstrate that the architect on the team can dramatically influence the reinvention. A city cannot be great without great architecture. You should not compromise the vision and its plan by building some meaningless project for the sake of building a "win". You must not build a project that has little architectural appeal. Build quality projects. As we have discussed, Bilbao is one of those reinvented cities that never deviated from building quality. There are numerous outstanding projects in downtown Bilbao, including the Frank Gehry-designed Guggenheim Museum, the footbridge over the Nervion River designed by Salvador Calatrava, the metro designed by Norman Foster, the Iberdrola Office Tower designed by Cesar Pelli, the new airport by Calatrava, and many other notable architects, including Zaha Hadid,

Lincoln Road garage. Miami Beach, Florida. Herzog and De Mueron, Architect

Phillippe Starck, and Arata Isozaki. Other cities have demanded high quality architecture in both civic and private buildings, and have been rewarded for creating a community of great design, even if what they design is controversial. Miami Beach is one such city, and it is not only attractive to visitors for its renovation of historical buildings—mostly modern hotels—but also now for its design of parking garages. Most of its recent public and public/private garages are designed by famous architects. Tours are even held in Miami Beach to visit those garages!

Team Members will Change

Recognize that change will cause dissension, which is the evil partner in the process of reinventing a city. Some members of the team may attempt to sabotage the vision to the extent that the leader or executive implementer may need to make changes to the team. Leaders must give and take—give direction and take away the dissenters and negative personalities. A leader must infuse new blood and energy throughout the reinvention period.

4
THE PLAN

A favorite saying in our firm is "PLAN YOUR WORK, THEN WORK YOUR PLAN." Making a plan is the fourth step to reinventing your city. It's not a new or overly scientific concept, but it's a MUST if you are going to be successful and stay on track. We can't tell you how many times we've watched employees work their tails off weeks on end, and still be behind schedule or not meet their deadlines. This happens because, without a very clear direction of how you will spend your day, you will waste time.

Magnify that issue on a broader scale for a city trying to implement change, and you have a recipe for disaster, or at best, epic inefficiency.

It's compounded when the entire city operates in a reactive mode and the city manager finds him or herself making decisions based on daily fires that pop up, as opposed to a long-term, goal-oriented direction to achieve a vision. A more classic case of lack of planning sometimes comes from the political arena—a mayor or commissioner who changes course every time a group of residents decides something needs to be done about something important to them. Perhaps it's a traffic light, or installing a speed bump or planting a street tree. Suddenly, the city staff is busy fixing these issues, jumping from one priority to another. The end result: a department which can't meet deadlines because the direction keeps changing at the top. Such situations are going to happen.

But, with a clear vision, supported by a detailed plan, change will indeed occur in spite of the distractions.

Watch out for those big, thick strategic plans with 1,000 goals, however. Really effective strategic plans are simple and tell a story of what the city will become. They are not a laundry list that comes out of a two-day planning session. An effective plan's goals should be pared down to one page and each department director should see that page so often it becomes the creed by which he or she operates.

Charleston's Mayor Riley told us that his city is still being guided by the plan they created back in the '70s, albeit with some updates and modifications. Originally, the Chamber of Commerce determined that something needed to be done. They hired a team and identified major issues that needed attention.

An historic plan was created that zeroed in on key markets and the exceptional buildings already existing in the quaint city.

Riley noted that the plan emphasized the following key topics:

1. Redevelopment of the commercial areas
2. Neighborhood redevelopment—"A healthy downtown needs healthy neighborhoods helping to restore and renovate them and affordable housing."
3. Making the city safe

Two other areas of emphasis were tourism management, and the now-famous Charleston waterfront that didn't become famous until Riley's efforts took hold. "You have to listen, and learn and keep the plan updated," Riley said.

It's also not enough to just have a plan. It has to be a plan that articulates the vision, provides written details about implementation, describes the strategies that will be needed for implementation, identifies funding sources and estimates the costs for each project contained in the plan. Many well-intended plans end up sitting on a shelf in some government office and never get implemented. A successful plan must be book-ended by the vision on the front end and the right implementation structure on the back end.

This principle bears repeating, because it's crucial to reinvention success:

> *The only way a plan will work is if the right vision is established in the first place. This means a vision that includes innovative and creative concepts, ones that will excite and inspire humans to respond. On the back end, the most innovative and creative plan is useless if the right talent isn't hired to implement it. Finally, having clear articulated strategies and directions for each implementation task are vital to an effective plan.*

To further clarify, this step to reinventing your city is not about having a city-wide plan to make sure residents are happy with their trash pickup or code enforcement. Those city-wide strategic plans are good, and every city needs them. This plan is about a *specific vision* for a *specific area* with *specific directions* to get the area to CHANGE. You'll still need to assess some city functions to understand how your plan fits into the city's operations, but don't get bogged down in city issues when drafting a reinvention plan. Once the overall plan is written, it is also useful to have discrete subsets of the plan to guide implementation through not only the long term, but the short term as well. Typically, we develop a five-year strategic implementation plan once the overall plan is in place and use that five-year plan as our daily guide.

When we met with Alfonso Martinez Cearra from Metropoli-30, the entity that largely drove the innovation portion of the impressive revitalization of Bilbao, he shared an interesting story about creating context for a plan.

He explained that although it's important to determine what current residents and stakeholders want their city to be, there is a whole population that isn't in the city yet that you are going to attract. Those additional residents—business owners, property owners, stakeholders, and others—are the key to the future, and you must take time to identify their goals and desires as well.

"A city is a group of people who believe in the future of their community," Alfonso said. "But a city is also about those who are not always there, or not in the city yet."

Because a city's future is measured in time, Alfonso said, "Consider the situation where a man raises a daughter. It takes years to raise her, then she grows up and meets a man and gets married, and has children with the man. The man is not from your family, and he wasn't there in the beginning, but he does become your future. So make the city for those who are coming, not just for those who are here. It will create a stronger family unit. Translated to a grander scale, it will make the fabric of a community stronger for all residents when you consider who may come to the city in the future and join those who are already there."

Jeff Koon's Puppy. Bilbao, Spain

Alfonso disliked surveys. "They're USELESS," he emphatically preached. "They're stupid, too. Asking a seventeen-year old-what they want the city to be is different from what a retiree will say." What are you going to do, write a plan to satisfy both? That's what some cities do and some plans are clearly a compilation of wants from multiple vantage points, or special interests."

Instead, he suggested, focus on a certain group of people that will be important to the future you are trying to create. In Bilbao's case, it was the children. "Children are the missing link in innovation," Alfonso said.

As he was telling us the story of how Bilbao got the Guggenheim Museum and how wonderful it was, he told us what he believed was the real coup. Alfonso believed Bilbao's real triumph was getting Jeff Koon's "Puppy"—the 60-foot-high flowered topiary that sits right outside the museum. Alfonso observed that many adults want to go to the Guggenheim, but few children will pull on their mothers' skirts dragging them there. The children will, however, drag their parents to see Puppy and end up at the museum. So, at an early age, children of Bilbao are exposed to the cultural and educational experiences a museum offers.

The children's playground at the rear of the museum was also built for that reason, and the combination of uses has brought spectacular results. "Puppy" is an excellent example of imagining who will be part of the future as you create an innovative plan for your city.

Master Plans Versus Redevelopment Plans

There is a difference between a "master plan" and a "redevelopment implementation plan." And there are reasons some plans end up sitting on a shelf while other plans are implemented. Plans sit on shelves because they are incomplete. We have always had a bit of a riff with consulting firms who simply write one-dimensional plans. Because engineers, architects and planners write most of these "master plans," there is usually a serious slant toward their own particular discipline. A consultant who is hired to write a master plan should really call it what it is—a zoning plan, or a design plan, or a right-of-way plan. The problem is that very few of these master plans include a meaningful real estate or market perspective, and more importantly, often lack innovation.

For example, if an architectural firm creates a plan that contains great recommendations for street improvements, garage locations, and design guidelines for new buildings, but fails to consider whether the recommendations will be embraced by the private sector or whether property owners will sell their land to make the plan work, then very likely only the public sector portions of the plan will get implemented. City personnel will scratch their heads wondering why the private sector isn't participating in the redevelopment.

In one city we know, the community argued for months over the design of a roadway running alongside the beach. The existing road was straight and parallel to the beach, but some folks wanted a large curve that would bulb out enough to allow a restaurant to be built right on the beach with the road curving behind it.

After countless hours of debate and fussing over design, the final plan curved the road. The architect didn't check with the engineers, however, and no one had checked with anyone else about whether there were any other issues with the curved roadway design. Imagine the dismay when everyone learned that there was more than $1 million worth of underground utilities in the area that would have to be relocated and there was nowhere to relocate them. All the design efforts and lengthy debate were for naught. The road is now built, and it's straight. The curved roadway plan, meanwhile, is gathering dust.

Plans also sit on shelves because the right people with the skill sets to create a plan are not hired. It may sound obvious, but simply being in the planning department or redevelopment department does not qualify someone to write a reinvention plan. As we explained in Chapter 3, the core team, and ultimately the full implementation team, will be the authors of an achievable plan to turn your city around.

Creating a plan that will guide reinvention is impacted not only by the skill sets of the team, it also is affected by external conditions that must be understood and appreciated. Here's a partial list of the skill sets and external conditions we have observed:

Being Innovative—Being able to define innovation and its impact to an area. (try it; it's hard to do well.) This is difficult because innovation depends on the unique characteristics of the area or city; it also depends on the lens by which such unique characteristics are viewed. The team members responsible for being innovative have to view the city or the area with a lens that sees unlimited possibilities and what the impact of those possibilities will have on the area they are viewing.

Having Vision and Being a Futurist—Being able to "see" things that are not there. Some people can drive through a blighted area and really see the future. We refer to these people as "futurists" and that is exactly what they are. It's not just about seeing the old buildings with new paint, or envisioning how the roadway will look after a streetscape project. It's about seeing the types of activity that will be taking place and seeing who and what will be there that isn't there now.

Understanding Real Estate and Market Conditions—All the visioning in the world won't help if you can't make sense of the real estate market in a given area. Just because an economist drafted a report on supply and demand doesn't mean the people who own buildings in the area are going to lease to the tenants you so desperately want to attract. And if the real estate market doesn't support your lofty plan, it's not going to happen. Someone on the team needs to be able to translate the real estate aspect of a plan into specific and realistic tasks that can be accomplished. Make sure to include lenders in the equation: are banks lending to small businesses, to large multi-family builders, to office developers? Don't design an office park if the lenders have determined that they won't take the risk in that area of your city.

Understanding Politicians and Managing the Slippery Slope of Politics—All cities have elected officials and political gadflies. There's no getting around them. The people who create and implement plans have to be able to navigate the political peaks and valleys without letting the politicians and gadflies hinder their job. That means being able to stay above the political fray and simply exercise good judgment and present sound business recommendations to those who vote. After that, get out of the way. Be prepared, however, to become a target for people who don't want change. They will go to the mayor or city commissioners and try to get rid of anyone involved in implementation. Elected officials need to continuously support the reinvention effort (no matter how politically unpopular) or the whole effort will grind to a halt.

Understanding "Dysfunctional" City Hall—Most city halls are like dysfunctional families. The sooner you accept this premise, the better off you will be. There is usually some form of alpha male or female positioning going on, and someone who is a malcontent trying to disrupt the effectiveness of somebody else. There's usually enough miscommunication to launch a war, and the silent treatment is often used between departments to see who will cry uncle first. And inevitably, there's someone ganging up on someone else. Those are just the moderately dysfunctional cities. The ones who let crazy residents drive the bus and dictate the city's future have even more dysfunctional dynamics. Suffice it to say, team members have to be able to maneuver around the dysfunction while creating "CHANGE." The best scenario is when there is a strong manager or other leader in city hall who insists on good communication, accountability and a team approach.

Understanding the Rules—The laws and regulatory options available to creating and implementing the plan are important; the person running the show needs to understand them. Can you speak zoning well enough to get the planning director to stop torturing the little restaurant that's simply trying to get a sidewalk café permit? Do you speak legalese enough to avoid letting the city attorney always tell you no? Do you speak enough engineering to stop the city engineer from making an eight-lane highway down Main Street? The best option is to have city departments embrace the plan; regardless, you have to see things from their viewpoints to know when they are being professional, and when they are simply creating arbitrary obstacles. Then, you have to be brave enough to say something and do everything you can to change the current way of doing business.

Being VERY Strategic—Some of the most technically skilled individuals don't have an ounce of strategic thinking; in the reinvention business, they will not succeed. You must stay one step ahead of everyone, and the only way to do that is to constantly strategize about your next move. Think like you're playing a game of chess.

Understanding Urban Design—This is obvious, and anyone implementing a plan can hire professionals. The more skills you have in urban design, however, the better you will shape the physical form of the reinvention plan.

Being the Ultimate Salesman—Reinvention is largely about convincing people to: 1) see something that isn't there yet through your vision; and 2) believe that it really will happen. Most of the time you are coming in on the heels of many years of nothingness and inactivity and frustration is very high. No one believes that "this time" it's really going to happen. You have to sell them, or at least keep them quiet long enough to do your thing. In Pompano Beach, there was a long-time businessman who owned a lot of properties and really had a bad attitude. When we told him what our plans were, he laughed and said, "Don't you know where you are? You're in 'PompaNO!' The city always says NO! And they can't do anything right . . . so NO! . . . I don't think your plans and vision will work." He was so nasty and negative. We told him we would prove him wrong. And, we would do it in twenty-four months. He was a royal pain in the backside for those twenty-four months; but, to his credit, he called one day and said, "OK, you were right. It's changing here, and I can't say that stuff anymore." He also moved to another state.

Plan Contents

All plans should include some basic components, but for successful reinvention to occur, there are several absolutes that must be included. We often get asked,

"How did you redevelop that area?" Or, "Where do we start?" Below are the components that we consider in every reinvention plan we create.

I. An Innovative Concept
II. Situation Analysis
III. Specific Objectives and Goals
IV. Key Strategies
V. Specific Tactics
VI. Budget
VII. Evaluation

An Innovative Concept

Being innovative is being able to see and describe something new and different, as well as the impact such innovations will have on the target area. What will the place "feel" like? What will people be "doing"? What will people be "saying" about the area once it's turned around? Answering these questions will lead to articulating an innovative concept. The innovative concept is what will draw people in and want the plan implemented so they can enjoy the experiences the innovations offer.

Situation Analysis

This plan component contains a frank assessment of the issues—strengths, weaknesses, opportunities and threats.

- **The urban form and physical attributes:** Remember that one of the three most important attributes a city needs to make people want to live there, according to the Knight Foundation/Gallop Poll, is "physical environment," including streets, rights-of-way, sidewalks, walkability, lighting, ease of finding their way around, points of interest, signage, landscaping, public areas and plazas, gathering places, parks and spots to stop, sit and enjoy, architecture, and safety.

- **The business and residential environment:** What types of businesses are there? Do they service the downtown or neighborhood? Are the businesses compatible? For example, are there chemical supply stores in the downtown core that are not compatible with retail? How far do you have to drive to get to a good grocer? Is there a food desert? Are the stores well-maintained? Is the signage a mess? Is there a large vacancy rate? Is there a lack of investment in general? What are the demographics? Can they support the desired types of businesses? If not, what has to happen to change that? What's the status of the housing stock? What's the percent of home ownership versus rental? What's the competition from neighboring cities?
- **The public environment:** Although city-wide issues aren't usually directly under the purview of a redevelopment program or initiative, they will affect the ability to "sell" the city to the private sector, be it a small mom-and-pop pizza shop, or a large, downtown corporate user. These factors must be considered and somehow dealt with in the plan.
- **Residents and their needs:** Are there enough parks and recreational activities for the residents? Are there neighborhoods that are clearly defined and desirable? Are the trash and utility services up to par? Is the city business-friendly? Is City Hall dysfunctional? Does the city have a bad reputation? Is the city safe?

Specific Objectives and Goals

Once the situation has been analyzed, the next step is to use that information to set specific goals and objectives. For example, if the situation analysis indicates the downtown has a high vacancy rate, and that condition is attributable to a perception that the downtown is unsafe, then the goal is to change the perception. Or, if there is actual crime, the objective is to reduce the criminal activity.

Key Strategies

These are the most important action items within the plan. If the issues are clearly defined and the goals or objectives are clearly established, the plan can still fail if the right strategies aren't employed. Using our previous example, the issue is the vacancy rate in the retail area. Simply putting a strategy in place to attract businesses won't work because of the additional issue involving a perception of crime. The strategy, then, must do double duty and deal with both issues simultaneously. Just dealing with the crime alone won't result in redevelopment. It is important to analyze the situation very carefully and be accurate as to: 1) what's in the way of redevelopment; and 2) what is an opportunity to capitalize on?

Specific Tactics

Specific tactics are the "devils in the details." If you don't have a specific, actionable item that someone is going to implement, the strategy will not go anywhere. Our strategy in the Northwood neighborhood of West Palm Beach was to: 1) hire a security firm; 2) promote the area as an up-and-coming Bohemian village where one-of-a-kind, eclectic boutiques were going to locate; and 3) partner with local bankers and real estate brokers to change their negative perceptions of the area, and to persuade them to join us in attracting new business to the area.

One warning: when you start to write specific tactics in a plan, and put budget amounts to them, this section can get bogged down, and can even become controversial. Suddenly, everyone has a cousin or friend who needs work, or has an old colleague who has opened a graphic design firm that should do the promotional materials for the marketing campaign. Or worse, residents will resist spending funds in the downtown when their neighborhoods need so much work. Staying focused on the vision and the specific objectives and goals will help your team resist these diversions.

Budget

A detailed description of the costs associated with each project or tactic, as well as the funding sources, should form the basis for the plan budget. This aspect of the plan is so significant, that we include more detail in Chapter 7, when we discuss Step Seven, financing the plan. We prefer using a "source and use" budget format. A source and use budget defines the funding sources and amounts of money available to fund the plan, and defines how much will be spent on each project and program. These types of budgets are very transparent and enable the general public to see exactly how much money is being invested to implement the plan. We recognize, however, that cities often have their own budgeting styles.

Evaluation

Although "evaluation" is not an actual written section of the plan, it is none the less a critical plan requirement. At the end of each fiscal or calendar year, analyze the results of the previous year's work related to the goals you set in the implementation plan. Eliminate programs that are not producing results and move funds to those areas that are gaining traction and meeting your specific goals and objectives. This is the time to revise those goals and objectives to better reflect new market conditions if necessary. Don't be afraid to state that a project or program was not successful and needs to be stopped or modified.

The Plan: A Case Study
Northwood Village, West Palm Beach, Florida

Northwood Village is a single element of a larger redevelopment plan we are implementing for the City of West Palm Beach. This element, however, is useful to illustrate how a well-developed plan works, even for a single element. This case study follows the plan contents and applies the plan to the Northwood Village reinvention.

I. Innovative Concept

Northwood Village was formerly a small business and neighborhood center for the northern portion of the city slated for redevelopment. The residents simply wanted it back to the way it was. The neighborhood businesses had morphed into uses that weren't compatible with any form of neighborhood center, so a complete change of concept was needed. The owner of a company that made boat canvasses and sewed large sails for sailboats owned a lot of property, and he didn't see anything wrong with his "retail." No amount of cajoling would convince him that a boat canvass maker would be better off in the industrial area. The innovative approach was to change the concept of a business and neighborhood center, and to concentrate on reinventing an environment for all things creative and cultural, with food and beverage as supportive uses. So, we were targeting businesses that weren't there yet, as well as people who would visit Northwood Village to experience something they couldn't experience anywhere else.

Northwood Village before any retailers had arrived. The city created the illusion of activity to demonstrate what a revitalized street should look like. West Palm Beach, Florida

Northwood Village after restaurants and shops were successfully attracted to the area. Over 130 businesses have opened. West Palm Beach, Florida

II. Situation Analysis

Formally called the Northwood Business District, the six-block, low-density, retail-oriented area included three parallel streets that connected the north and south end of the city. The area had gone into a twenty-year, slow decline, and the combination of vacant store fronts, tired and poorly maintained buildings, a spattering of industrial sites, storefront churches, lack of interest from property owners or merchants, and nearby prostitution, left the area desolate.

2a. Strengths
- Good street grid
- Good retail frontage and potential for remerchandising
- A handful of interested property owners and merchants
- Incentives available to assist with facade programs

2b. Weaknesses
- Apathy among merchants and property owners
- Perception of crime
- High investment risk for new business owners

2c. Opportunity
- Nearby merchants looking to expand
- Interest by the elected officials to change the area
- Funds available for improvements

2d. Threats
- Economy
- Crime
- Apathy

III. Specific Objectives and Goals
- Reduce the perception of the area being unsafe from 48% to 20% in one year.
- Attract ten new businesses in one year
- Rebrand the area as a fun, exciting place with eclectic shops and a Bohemian feel.

IV. Key Strategies
- Create a comprehensive campaign that includes a combination of security, marketing and outreach to the key partners needed to attract new businesses, namely, bankers and real estate brokers. The very visible security officers would also double as "Neighborhood Ambassadors." This approach will not only provide the safety element, but will downplay and de-emphasize the apparent need for security. As ambassadors, they act as community representatives.
- To attract new businesses, rebrand the area from Northwood Business District to Northwood Village. Create a new logo and look for the area, with design guidelines for shops and buildings and streetscape elements. This will support rebranding of the area as a Bohemian village, where one-of-a-kind, eclectic shops and restaurants would want to locate. Activities will include cold calls, preparing leasing

packages, public relations stating the area is going to change, and networking with the real estate brokerage community.
- Hold a banker/broker event inviting area banking professionals who make small business loans, as well as real estate agents in the area who lease retail space. Create a story board about what the area will become and print materials they can take with them to reinforce the new image and brand for the area.
- Hold monthly "Art & Wine" promenades to get people used to visiting the area.
- Prepare streetscape improvements to enhance the physical environment, and provide facade improvements to spruce up the businesses.

V. & VI. Specific Tactics and Budget

Hire two guards during hours when events are held and visitors are in the area	$75,000
Create marketing materials, including new logo and print materials	$3,000
Host banker/broker event	$500
Monthly Art & Wine promenades	$12,000
Streetscape improvements	$500,000
Facade improvement funds	$60,000

VII. Evaluation

Each implementation plan will have a unique set of priorities and fund balances to work with. Therefore, analyzing the effectiveness of the previous year's expenditures varies. In our Northwood Village example, the emphasis was on streetscape improvements and security. The investments were supposed to improve the aesthetics of the street and reduce the perception that the area was unsafe. In this case, surveys showed that the community liked the redesigned street environment and they felt safer. No additional funds were needed for street improvements the following year; however a continued security presence was needed to maintain the safe environment. Generally, the goal is to secure as much funding as possible in the beginning stages of reinvention and apply the funds to the specific projects that will have the most significant impact.

The Plan: Unanticipated Success

If a city wants to change an area, there must be a solid, yet flexible, plan that everyone agrees will result in the vision being met. There can be twists to the implementation, however, and the history of how Times Square got redeveloped is a perfect example. The plan for Times Square was terrific—a grand plan with a clear vision, but the Times Square implementers didn't end up using the plan! It worked anyway because the plan vision was so clear, even though another form of implementation was used to redevelop the area. That's not necessarily a problem, and the fact that the original plan wasn't used doesn't detract from the project's eventual success.

The original vision was for a grand-scale redevelopment project, which is what ultimately occurred. Some say it turned out better than anyone could have imagined. What is important, however, is that there was a plan, and it had a vision behind it.

Because it has been decades since Times Square was in such a deteriorated state, many people might not even recall a Times Square that was anything but a vibrant, state-of-the-art destination for the world to visit. In the early 1980s, though, Times Square was a sleazy, crime-ridden, blighted section of the city dominated by prostitutes and pornographers, who made it so seedy, only patrons of the illicit trades would venture there.

Reinvention of Times Square needed three things: tax abatement, rezoning and policing. A group called the Urban Development Corporation (UDC) put together a massive initiative to revitalize Times Square that included a $2.6 billion plan that would extend tax abatement deals to developers and encourage them to transform Times Square by building grand office towers, a huge merchandise market, a fancy hotel, and by restoring historic theaters and revamping the dingy 42nd Street subway station. Others sponsoring the plan were Mayor Ed Koch, and in the background, *The New York Times*, whose headquarters gave the square its name at the turn of the century.

The lawless climate and unsavory imagery that was cast in news articles had produced devastating economic consequences. In 1984, the entire 13-acre area on which the UDC was focused employed only 3,000 people in legitimate businesses. The tax base was under $10 million.

No bona fide business was going to become a pioneer and open shop in such a blighted area. Lined with single-room occupancy hotels and massage parlors, greasy spoons and pornographic bookstores, the street only attracted junkies, johns, hookers and pimps.

The UDC plan was enormous in scale, with Times Square as the centerpiece, surrounded by over 4 million square feet of giant office towers. A real estate group was offered a $240 million tax abatement to build new office space, and they hired a renowned architectural team. The massive plan also called for a 2.4 million square foot computer and garment-wholesale mart, as well as a 500-room luxury hotel with additional office and retail space. The historic theaters would get a multimillion dollar spruce-up and reopen as nonprofit cultural centers. The project was capped off with a $100 million major makeover of the 42nd Street subway station. As with many plans, the folks leading the redevelopment team thought the entire project had to be done at one time in order to create enough momentum to drive the blight and sleaze away.

And that is where it apparently all came to a stop. The plan faded and the construction contemplated by UDC never began.

The Times Square initiative became the same type of victim to the real estate market as was just experienced by others when the market bubble ended so dramatically in 2008 and ultimately resulted in the great recession. At the time, the commercial real estate market was already beginning to peak in 1984 and the stock-market crash of 1987 finished it off.

Often, as seen in other real estate market cycles, it's at the worst of times that brave investors take risks that sometimes pay off. In 1990, Viacom signed a lease on Broadway, and other major firms started to follow, including Morgan Stanley.

Disney subsequently came along, and with a $25 million government-issued loan, rehabbed the New Amsterdam Theater. By 1995, AMC, the entertainment giant, moved to the neighborhood, and Madame Tussaud's Wax Museum opened a Times Square branch. Developers started to take note.

So, what happened that drew the private sector back? Was it simply that the market crash had created a real estate opportunity, or was there more to it? Clearly, the city and its redevelopment arm weren't able to spark the development, but it was starting anyway. In this case, the city did do three key things that helped to move the redevelopment forward: 1) the government tackled the crime issue and started to aggressively fight back; 2) it kicked the sex industry out of the area; and 3) it targeted big businesses willing to locate in the area, and supported them with tax and other government subsidies. Slowly, the image of Times Square changed from sleazy, blighted, and drug-ridden to one that had huge potential and tremendous investment opportunities.

While the redevelopment plan did not unfold as UDC envisioned, the plan nevertheless laid the foundation for changing Times Square. Reducing taxes for businesses willing to locate in the neighborhood, offering a combination of tax abatements, low-interest loans, and other subsidies that attracted new business were BIG incentives and those incentives paid off. The $250 million in tax incentives resulted in over $2.5 billion in private sector investment.

In trying to review the plan's effectiveness, it's hard to determine what the 42nd Street Development Plan really achieved in terms of influence. Some of the envisioned projects did get built, but many were not conceived or anticipated in the plan. It did do what all plans must do. It created a vision and a focal point for the conversation about how to turn the area around. In the case of Times Square, it was not as much about the path itself, as it was about the destination.

5

IMPLEMENTATION

Step five to reinventing your city—implementation—does not provide instant gratification. You will experience short term successes along the way, but implementation is a lengthy process that can take as long as twenty five years for a full cycle. Implementation follows articulation of the vision, having a leader who steps forward and takes the reins, assembling the core team and making a plan. Implementation is the step that involves actually working the plan. It is boots on the ground, doing the job, painting, paving, planting, building and rebuilding. Implementation is the step that has its bright periods, such as when the unlit, unattractive road becomes a beautiful, illuminated streetscape filled with inviting street furniture and landscaping that transforms a neighborhood; and, implementation is the step that can be fraught with events and people that can derail the process.

At the beginning of the implementation phase, nothing has been built and the clock is ticking. The leader has probably spent over a year up to this point, and he is beginning to get questions at public meetings, such as: "By the way, mayor, how is it going? You know, your vision for making big changes in the city?" The leader may turn to the executive implementer and say: "OK, now is the time to get something done! Stop planning and let's proceed to implementation."

Don't be silent during the implementation start-up; citizen chatter will fill the silence. And, critics can sometimes paralyze the initial implementation effort. As implementation commences, changes will begin to occur, gradually at first, and increasing over time. There will be supporters of the implementation, but there will also be naysayers. Sometimes, the naysayers stand on the sidelines and criticize the actual work. They even call the mayor about minor imperfections or something they consider out of order. The leader and the executive implementer should spend as much time as needed to keep the public well-informed at each phase of implementation. And, as Mayor Graham illustrated in Chapter 2 with the historic church, choose your battles wisely. If there is sufficient citizen opposition to some aspect of the implementation, try to find a creative solution that is consistent with the vision but that doesn't stop working the plan.

Critics, however, can sometimes paralyze the implementation effort. This is where some cities, unfortunately, lose momentum. Loss of momentum will continue if the plan is sitting in the wrong office. For example, if the plan lives with the planners, implementation may be hindered by the fact that they are rule makers and rule enforcers. Typically, there is no one in the planning department that can serve as the leader or the executive implementer. In contrast, the Charleston plan lived in the right place. Mayor Joe Riley still keeps his original plan in his bookcase opposite his executive desk.

Implementation success hinges on very finely tuned execution by the full team of professional implementers. There are a whole host of scenarios that can affect implementation for better or worse. The following examples depict some of those scenarios and how they impact successful implementation.

Weak Executive Implementer

Failure to get implementation started may be the result of an unfocused and weak-kneed executive implementer. He or she may be a good thinker who is also good at putting a plan together. That is not enough. The executive implementer must be a doer, a pusher, a strategist, a leader of the team, and most importantly, he or she must not be deterred by public criticism. The executive implementer must be able to get the job done.

The Leader Departs

Trouble may arise if the implementation team loses the leader. It may be because of local political office term limits, or it may be due to public criticism. The leader must be in place a sufficiently long period of time so that implementation becomes a train that cannot be stopped. Delray Beach lost its leader, Mayor Doak Campbell, early in the process, and it was ten years before another leader emerged. That leader, Tom Lynch, reignited implementation of the plan. His efforts and those of his successors over the next twenty five years led to reinventing Delray Beach.

The Leader with Longevity

An effective leader who stays in place for a number of years can bring a lot to a city looking to turn itself around. Charleston Mayor Joe Riley remained in office for over forty years. Mayor Riley will turn over the reins to a new leader in 2016. Let's hope that Charleston will be as lucky again. Think of West Palm Beach, which has a mayoral election every four years, and term limits of eight years. First came Nancy Graham, who served eight years; then, a four-year period of continuing the Graham policies by one-term mayor, Joel Daves; then, Lois Frankel for eight years; and now, Jeri Muoio in her second four year term. Like Charleston, West Palm Beach was fortunate to have a series of focused leaders.

Similarly, Bilbao Mayor Azkuna was in office for fifteen years until his recent and untimely death in 2014. He was a master politician, a dominant figure in the Basque national political party, and an extremely effective leader. He had the enviable character trait of also being a compelling and charismatic speaker. This gave him a tremendous advantage in overseeing a powerful board (Bilbao Ria 2000) that voted on funding the first phase of downtown redevelopment projects. While Bilbao may be deemed a democracy, once a leader is elected as president, governor or mayor, the elected position is oftentimes dominated by the leader's political party. Mayor Azkuna was successful because he was able to control his party, and he used the fear of Basque nationalism as

Mayor Joe Riley. Charleston, South Carolina

a tool to convince the national government, which was once dominated by Castilians, to support his redevelopment vision. In Spain, it is often said that Madrid gave huge sums of money to rebuild Bilbao because it was a way to modernize the Basque nation. Rebuilding Bilbao was a better alternative than spending national funds to control Basque nationalism. Azkuna's longevity, combined with his initial dominance, enabled the reinventing of Bilbao and implementation of the plan.

New Leadership

New leadership can bring a different perspective to the plan underway or a desire to create a new plan altogether. The issue is always going to be how new leadership affects the vision, the plan and its implementation. Delray Beach went through a period of coasting along and resting on the successes of the previous administrations. Coasting along is a prescription for stagnation, and stagnation inevitably breeds the need for change. Delray Beach elected Cary Glickstein as mayor in 2014. Glickstein campaigned on crafting a new plan, without mention of rebuilding an implementation team once the plan was in place. Notably, a strong implementation team is needed any time a plan gets rewritten.

Full Implementation Team

The core team will consist of members with marketing, legal, urban design, project management, and financial skill sets. Rounding out the full implementation team may mean adding several project managers, engineers, event managers, administrative personnel, public relations, city planners, and economic development and real estate experts.

By the time a full implementation team is assembled, the leader must check that the original vision is still clear, check for adjustments in the plan, and not compromise the vision because of public opinion. Implementation may experience rough patches as changes are made in the city. All through the process of developing a vision and a plan, the leader must determine whether the executive implementer has the skill and stamina to proceed into the implementation phase.

What Does the Plan Say?

The question the implementation team must answer on day one is: what are the first tasks we need to tackle? The initial plan prepared by the core team provides the blueprint for the work that will be executed by the implementation team. The first plan should contain an overall physical master plan that describes the ideal targeted area, including pedestrian street design, parking, new community facilities, housing sites, central plaza design, and many other elements. Since the plan should not be constrained by what is not allowed under current rules (zoning), it may trigger the need to "change the rules" and amend the zoning code. So, new zoning legislation must be included in the implementation phase. The plan will also take into consideration the cost of redevelopment and should contain the first five-year projection of revenues and expenses, which is essentially the business plan for redevelopment. The implementation team will need the five-year strategic implementation plan as their daily guide. This five year plan will list the first items to be built, such as a pedestrian main street and municipal parking lots for the future wave of new consumers coming to the downtown. The five year strategic implementation plan is essential to starting the work.

There is some work, however, that is so self-evident that it can start immediately without the plan being completed and adopted officially. For example, Delray Beach started a four-block streetscape, rebuilding existing municipal parking lots, acquiring property for future redevelopment sites, and providing small business loans as a recruitment incentive to fill up the city's 500,000 square feet of vacant, downtown retail space. Remember that the leader may ask the executive implementer to start something even without the final five year strategic implementation plan in place. You can look for the low hanging fruit in the plan but don't fall victim to distractions.

Change the Rules and Regulations

The city planner, an expert in land use (comprehensive planning) and zoning, may need to change the zoning rules and regulations using the plan as its guide. The plan contains a physical concept of redeveloping an area, prepared by a set of urban designers, and shows the city planner what rules have to be changed. Often, city codes are based upon outdated suburban codes that are likely to thwart redevelopment. Important clues to watch out for are: high parking ratios; wide streets; excessive turn lanes; off-street parking rather than curb parking; narrow sidewalks; excessive setbacks; high open-space requirements; anti-urban landscape codes; artificially low density for residential; removal of on-street parking in order to add lanes to primary streets; and arbitrary height restrictions. Provisions for mixed-use development with commercial retail on the ground floor and residential or offices on upper floors rarely exist. So change the rules! If the new plan calls for seven-story, mixed-use buildings with ground-floor retail, as we enjoy in so many European cities, such as Barcelona and Paris, the city planner must then rewrite the code to allow such mixed-use. Alternatively, the implementation team can write the code for the planning department, who, in turn, will take the rewrite through the approval process.

In 2009, the City of Pompano Beach hired our firm as the executive implementers. We put together a core team and made a plan, which became the guide for the Pompano Beach full implementation team to follow. Mixed use was in the plan, but the code essentially prohibited mixed use redevelopment. In particular, the code did not allow residential use above commercial. The implementation team, together with the city's planning department, successfully rewrote the land use and zoning codes to allow mixed-use. The process took almost two years. It required the leader, Mayor Fisher to exert his political influence at the county level, as well as garner the needed approval from the Pompano Beach City Commission.

Bring the Planning Department into the Vision

In every city hall there is a planning and zoning department; the question to ask is whether the department's planners are on board with the vision? If they are not, the implementation team is going to have an uphill battle to change the existing rules. It is essential for the implementation team to spend time introducing the plan and convincing the existing planning department employees, particularly the director, to support the vision and the plan. The planning department needs to be a partner with the implementation team. The new plan will be about skinny streets, establishing or re-establishing a street grid, wide sidewalks, on-street parking, shade trees along the right-of-way, small neighborhood parks, social gathering places (plazas), shared parking, low parking ratios, setbacks that force urban development to move to the street, unleashing density to attract residential, lowering or eliminating open space requirements, raising the roof on building heights, and getting rid of drive-through, fast food, and other uses that don't promote reinvention. If the planning department resists the plan, overtly or subtly, the leader will need to step in and take the necessary measures to get the planning department's full support.

Bring the Building Department into the Vision

An implementation team's role is not only to plan; it is also to build, or encourage the private sector to build. Constructing buildings and tenant spaces requires building permits, which may sound simple. In some cities, obtaining building permits can be very frustrating. If the private sector is doing the building, the implementation team's role will be to facilitate getting permits as efficiently as possible so construction is not delayed. This is particularly important if it is a restaurant that's being built. By their nature, restaurants have building code requirements that other uses don't share. Getting a restaurant from permit to grand opening as quickly as possible is essential because, as we have already seen, restaurants will fuel downtown redevelopment, particularly in the early years of implementation. Make sure you bring the building department into the redevelopment mission. Building codes may seem straightforward, but humans make them much more complicated.

Bring the Police Department into the Vision

An implementation team is likely going into distressed neighborhoods and commercial districts where crime is out of control and buildings are blighted. What role should the police have in implementing the vision? An extremely important one. The police must take charge of changing the image of slum and blight by reducing and eliminating the fear of crime. Otherwise, consumers will never dare to venture into an area they fear. What will a consumer do if, on their first visit to a new restaurant in a blighted area, their automobile is vandalized or a panhandler approaches them? They will never come back. The police must prepare the area with a strong presence prior to any new development. Let the criminals and loiterers know that the police are on board with the new development and they are taking control of the area. And, if the police are not willing to buy into the vision, then private security must take their place. For example, in West Palm Beach, the implementation team was successful in attracting many new businesses to

Northwood Village, including restaurants, retailers, and clothing stores. A police presence was essential to the success of the redevelopment, and the implementation team hired additional private, 24/7 security, which proved to be invaluable to deterring crime and attracting new business.

Beautify the Streets

The urban design team member leads the effort to develop the physical plan, which will contain very specific concepts for making beautiful streets that are suitable for walking. Two members of the team—the engineer and the urban designer—together select the first streets to improve. In many cases, downtowns have laid idle since World War II. Some downtowns still remain idle after a failed beautification. Street beautification is essential to the initial implementation. A small stretch of beautiful, pedestrian streets will assist your economic development manager in attracting new businesses. Focus on a small area, say four blocks, as did Delray Beach and West Palm Beach, and then work outward from there. Most cities today are still unattractive because during the post-war period, cities concentrated on the vision of building suburbs. Downtowns emptied and downtown maintenance was eliminated from city budgets. In today's world, however, beautiful streets attract new businesses and new residents.

In Delray Beach, a four-block area was beautified and all the pedestrian-friendly above and below ground improvements were made. The project cost approximately $1 million dollars per block. Merchants howled, however: "No oak trees! They will block the view of our signs." The leader said, "No. The oak trees stay in." The leader recognized that the street would someday contain pedestrians and the oak trees would shade the shoppers and the cafe tables and provide a buffer to the traffic. It's true that the oak trees, until they are taller, might partially block the view of store signs, but those viewers are in automobiles, not walking on the sidewalk.

Street beautification is not the only answer to redevelopment, but it is one tool to use in the reinvention process. In the case of Delray Beach, it took approximately five years before the pedestrians showed up to enjoy the

Las Ramblas, one of the greatest urban sidewalks attracts millions of visitors every year. Barcelona, Spain

Atlantic Avenue. Delray Beach, Florida

new streets. Visiting Delray Beach today, you would think that some event is taking place every night. The event is urban city life, and it occurs every day in this city of 60,000+ people. Why did it take five years for pedestrians to come after the street beautification? First, there were no people living downtown, and second, there were no mixed-use buildings. Early pedestrians had to be imported from the neighborhoods surrounding downtown and from neighboring cities. They came in automobiles to dine at the new, upscale restaurants. The executive implementer recruited a dozen or more restaurants of high quality that attracted Delray Beach locals, neighboring cities' locals and tourists during the winter.

Seasonal business does not sustain an economy for long. All businesses need a year-around demand in order to survive. Once Delray Beach was able to attract multi-family developers to build in the downtown, then the retail establishments were able to sustain themselves year-round.

Atlantic Avenue. Delray Beach, Florida

Urban Parks

Every neighborhood, whether it is a block or a set of blocks, needs a park. Parks are where residents socialize, walk their dogs, play with their children and grandchildren, and where citizens, both residents and visitors, can take a breather. Most city zoning codes forget about urban parks and most city redevelopment agencies are always trying to buy property and save funds to build urban parks. The private sector is expected to pitch in and help build parks as well. Urban parks can be as small as Paley Park in New York City (one brownstone lot), or as large as full city blocks. Urban parks are not intended to be used by everyone; rather, they are intended for the residents within walking distance, and, typically, no more than two blocks away. For a small investment, less than a condominium swimming pool, urban parks provide enormous enjoyment to residents and visitors. An urban park can even allow a small café to have tables and chairs for morning coffee, lunch and dinner. Be proactive. Change the zoning or building codes to require that new construction contribute funds, or land, to an urban park fund

In Bilbao, the city closed a street for two blocks in the financial district, and it became an urban, hardscape, tree-lined park. On each block, several restaurants secured permits to serve food in the closed-street park. A playground facility was built in the park, so that after work families could mingle together and have their kids play in the playground. Apartment and office buildings line the park. People can now enjoy a glass of wine and tapas, socialize with friends for an hour or more and have their kids play with classmates in the playground. Urban life can be very fulfilling in reinvented Bilbao.

Parking

A parking demand analysis, prepared by the core team, perhaps with the assistance of a parking consultant, will determine the level of parking demand based upon the projected build-out of the plan.

Parking demand should not be based upon the parking code, which will likely be changed. Suburban parking codes are not practical for a downtown,

Implementation 81

Neighborhood park. Bilbao Spain

Street plaza, after work. Bilbao, Spain

because parking is typically shared, and the public sector typically provides the majority of downtown parking. Particularly in mixed-use downtowns, parking is shared at different times of day, on different days of the week, and at different times of the year by residents, retail consumers, visitors and office users. Based upon the plan and the parking demand analysis, the implementation team may make immediate plans for increasing or improving the parking supply. A critical rule in downtown redevelopment, however, is that you must plan for new parking at least two years ahead of the demand, because it takes about two years to actually provide the supply. In the eyes of the consumer or visitor, you always want the appearance that there is an ample supply of parking. Avoid getting caught flat-footed with a string of new restaurants along your main street with nowhere for customers to park. And, even if the demand for parking doesn't quite keep up with new supply, prospective tenants looking at the downtown will be impressed when they see a new supply. The rule is: "Build parking before they come. If you don't, they will not come."

Transportation and Governmental Coordination

When we met with Max Jeleniewski in The Hague, he shared a copy of a guiding policy document called The Hague Policy on Traffic and Transport: Conscious Choices—Smart Organization. Note the emphasis on two concepts, conscious choices and smart organization. These are two important concepts to consider when making plans for roadways and transportation systems.

First, they didn't draft a plan based solely on existing rules and regulations. They made conscious choices about their hierarchy of needs; and pedestrians were at the top, not cars. All too often, county or state transit or transportation plans drive right of way designs that don't compliment a city's reinvention plans. In Florida, we have systems that measure traffic, and when the road gets a failing grade, we tend to make it wider. There's an inherent conflict between a county or state objective of moving traffic at any cost, and a city that's trying to create a pedestrian environment by narrowing the roadway. In some cases, the county or state will transfer ownership of the roadway to the city, and that offer is usually met with resistance because the city doesn't want the maintenance expense. That may be a penny wise and pound foolish approach, however. Cities need to analyze what the cost/benefit is and determine if they will lose more revenue by allowing the street to become uninhabitable for commerce, or assume the cost of owning and maintaining a roadway that attracts businesses and people.

Second, the concepts of ensuring there is an organizational structure in place for implementation ties back into our philosophy discussed in Chapter Three, The Team. Only when the right organizational system exists, do plans and programs get effectively implemented. Max quipped: "You can't ride a bike on a piece of paper." In other words, you better make sure you can build the bike lane, not just put in in a plan.

In addition to roadways, there must be a long range plan for transit or alternative modes of transportation. Larger transit systems are normally confined to large cities; however, all cities need to reflect on their transit and transportation options. The Hague had to retrofit their entire underground system to accommodate the new trams that were needed when they knocked down the large roadway system we talked about in Chapter Two. Don't just think about today, but 50 years from now, and what should be done to be prepared to enable good pedestrian movement.

City Parking Enterprise Fund

A few enlightened cities in the U.S. understand what a parking enterprise fund is. What it is not is a slush fund for the city to use as it sees fit as part of its general fund. It is, rather, a revenue source to meet existing, and ever-important future parking needs. Cities need to isolate parking revenue from the general fund. This will result in more parking for the downtown, which results in more business attracted to the downtown, which results in higher property values. Parking is an essential element in any economic redevelopment strategy. Without parking, new businesses will not invest their capital in their retail or office establishment.

84   Reinventing Your City

Parking garage. Pompano Beach, Florida

The future of city funds lies with attracting new real estate, which, in turn, sends tax dollars to the city's general fund.

As we saw in Chapter One, Pompano Beach established a parking enterprise fund that became a useful tool as it redeveloped its waterfront. While the initial implementation phase produced a beachfront surface parking lot containing 125 spaces, the enterprise fund will enable the city to complete the next phase, a 600-parking space multi-level garage.

Miami Beach operates its parking system like a business. It owns over 15,000 parking spaces, all of which are metered. The city owns seven parking garages and it joint-ventures with a very active real estate development industry to build parking garages. There are few public spaces in Miami Beach that do not charge for parking—even residential curb parking is metered. Its parking rates have trended upward over the years as demand has increased. However, its revenues pay for new parking garages when they are needed in a particular area of the city. The City of Miami Beach receives not only revenues from parking, but new tax revenue from all the new businesses attracted to the city.

Urban housing. Delray Beach, Florida

Housing

There is no more important land use in a downtown than housing, particularly housing projects filled with young consumers and boomers. Residents activate the streets, support the retailers and join the cultural institutions. Without them, you have no pedestrians, no customers, no life, no culture, and no sense of community. Don't count on the suburbanites to come to the downtown and act like locals. Suburban customers are fickle. Residents, in contrast, are usually in the downtown to stay. In Florida, try to convince a new urbanite in Miami to move to another city. Impossible! The suburban customers come occasionally, but if they represent an older population, their spending habits often will not sustain urban retailers. There is nothing worse than being in a downtown after 5 p.m. and there is no one on the street. In the 1980s, the local Delray Beach newspaper headlines said: "City declared dead after 5." Delray Beach came to life after 5 p.m. when parking became available, when streets were designed for pedestrians, when lighting was installed for the pedestrian and parkers, when housing was built in the downtown, when restaurants populated the main street, and when the city's central marketing management team held exciting events on main street, which made the street a fun place to be.

Restaurants and Retailers in the Downtown

Restaurants are essential to a vibrant downtown. They are a destination use. Restaurant-goers who initially arrive in automobiles often become the first pedestrians in an evolving downtown. In Delray Beach, which has over 100 restaurants in the downtown, it is now a market requirement to have an outdoor café. Interestingly, in the early 1990s, it was illegal to have an outdoor café on the main street. Delray Beach's implementation team changed the code. The restaurant industry in Delray Beach spurred interest, and consequently, another important retail use in a downtown emerged— women's apparel.

Remember the couple from Chicago who moved to Delray Beach? The Novaks frequented many restaurants on the main street. After dinner, Ana would tell her husband that they were going for a walk to window shop. Ana wanted to buy an outfit. Young entrepreneurs reintroduced the small store, retail apparel business. Today, Delray Beach has over forty shops, including a few that survived from the 1970s. Once you see at least one women's apparel store on a downtown block, you know that redevelopment has reached a certain mark of success. In 2014, Delray Beach saw its first national clothing retailers open shop on the main street: Urban Outfitters and BCBG.

Clean and Safe

The term "clean and safe" is the modern, urban phrase for well-maintained streets and a police presence. After the streets are beautified, they need to be well-maintained, and look as clean in the fifth year as they do the first day. And once pedestrians appear, there is a need for security. In fact, the security must be there before the pedestrians arrive. Delray Beach had the reputation of having part of their downtown on the "other side of the tracks."

Urban Outfitters. Delray Beach, Florida

Residents would often say that they would never venture west of the railroad. "It wasn't safe there."

Once the first brave pedestrians came—who, without realizing it, became the de facto security force—the city implemented a very important police reorganization plan. They divided the city into zones—the downtown being one such zone—and assigned two uniformed policemen into two daily shifts, patrolling on bicycles. This occurred in the 1990s and was called "community policing." It worked and was the brainchild of a very effective leader—the police chief. Today, the city's implementation team, the CRA, runs the city's Clean and Safe Program.

At 4 a.m. every morning, a cleaning crew starts their work, picking up trash, emptying garbage cans, and making notes on needed maintenance, such as irrigation sprinkler repairs. When the first consumer arrives at Starbucks at 5 a.m., you will not see a single cigarette butt on the street. Today, Clean and Safe is another modern utility as important as water, sewer and drainage for the downtown. We now expect that in our downtown the flowers are

Cleaning crew. Barcelona, Spain

blooming and everything looks clean. It should be that way, because, in fact, the street is our downtown living room.

Marketing

A comprehensive marketing and communication plan guides the promotional efforts for targeted districts or entire cities. Successful marketing programs attract consumers, enhance the sales of the existing restaurants, promote and attract retailers and infuse life into a city attempting to reinvent itself. Marketing is the effort by which a city attracts private investment to a targeted area. Successful implementation of the marketing element of a plan results in: new businesses, grand openings and ribbon cuttings!

The marketing members of the implementation team will understand what it takes to fill empty storefronts. They will understand how to create a brand, "sell" the vision to prospects and build upon a city's success to attract more businesses. Marketing plans are results driven. The implementation team will create a plan that includes: research and analysis; strategic

Dining on the Avenue: Downtown Delray Beach event

planning; business attraction and retention; public relations; creative services—place branding, campaign and consumer promotions, graphic design and copy writing; social media—website development, online strategies; special events, sponsorship and activating spaces; cultural facility program development and management; and trade show representation.

In Delray Beach, "Art and Jazz on the Avenue," an event that started with 1500 visitors in 1991, today brings over 30,000 people to the Delray Beach downtown. Similarly, in West Palm Beach, "Clematis by Night" in the downtown and "Art and Wine Promenade" in Northwood Village bring thousands of new visitors to the city for each event. We have already seen the power of branding when Oakland Park identified its brand as a culinary arts destination and the influx of new business that resulted.

Be on the lookout for opportunities to engage marketing partners to take over some of the operations and expenses. For example, the Delray Beach Downtown Marketing organization later called the "Marketing Cooperative," took charge of not only events, but also the maintenance of the brick sidewalks, public relations, advertising the downtown, promotion of nighttime retailing, way-finding, retail storefront redesign, and merchant education. Taking a cue from the extremely well-organized and effective indoor mall owners and managers, downtowns need to be run as an outdoor mall. Forming a marketing management team, as Delray Beach did, made a major impact on consumer attraction and, subsequently, business recruitment. And, the local residents of Delray Beach began to shop in their own city instead of going to the mall at a city next door.

Private Investment

Although Step Six in reinventing your city is discussed in detail in the next chapter, it is important to at least describe the implementation team's role in engaging the private sector. Successful implementation of this step forms the basis for changing the economics and the real estate valuation of an area of the city. It will involve: introducing the private sector to the vision; identifying opportunities for private sector participation; and removing barriers to private sector involvement. Understanding real estate valuation is a critical component of engaging the private sector. In the beginning stages of reinventing your city, the private sector will not be interested. Business attraction efforts, however, should begin the very first day and it should be a task for all members of the team.

The Delray Beach executive implementer assisted an undercapitalized businessman with financing to convert a 1930's downtown gas station into Elwood's Dixie Barbeque. The city's investment was $125,000 for the land and tenant improvements. Eighteen years later, the tenant sold the restaurant to an upscale vendor for over $1 Million. The result was a tremendous increase in the taxable value of the parcel and an overall increase to the tax base. Business attraction is an art, not suited for a person wanting a desk job. It requires personality and salesmanship, as well as research skills.

Market research identifies gaps in the market and uses this data to assist new and existing business with their product definition. A good implementation team will focus on recruiting the local commercial real estate brokers to assist with business attraction efforts and to facilitate speedy approvals of construction permits.

Don't capitulate to the sideline critics who call the mayor and suggest that the mayor attract a "home run" business to solve the economic woes of the city. While reinventing your city, it is hard to attract a "home run" and it is counter-productive to spend much time on such an endeavor. Only after the reinvention has reached a certain state will the home run businesses come to you. The mayor's message to the critics has to be: "We are not in the home run business. We first have to make a great city and then the home run business will come."

Redevelopment is accomplished building by building, address by address. Ten new businesses on a typical city block have far more economic impact in the long run than one new big box home run.

Financing the Plan

The implementation team has a number of significant responsibilities in connection with financing the plan. They will be required to identify available sources of funding to finance the plan. They must strategically identify the projects and programs that will immediately begin the reinvention process based on the amount of funding available. Because another goal is to leverage any available funding, the implementation team members must understand financing mechanisms, such as issuing bonds, short term loans, private placement and other lender-driven financing tools, and capitalizing on real estate investments. Technical skills are needed to be able to access and deploy the money, with the attendant accountability.

Schedule

A schedule for implementation of the plan is essential. Clearly defined benchmarks, deadlines, action items and the person in charge should all be part of the schedule. The implementation team members must understand all elements of the schedule and take ownership of any tasks assigned to them, individually. A schedule will detail short term and long term projects. As we have discussed, reinventing your city can be a lengthy process. The schedule should also recognize that over time market conditions and other circumstances will change the existing conditions. While it is important to maintain the integrity of the schedule, it will be necessary to make adjustments from time to time.

The Delray Beach schedule that follows reveals the ebb and flow of the market conditions relative to retail reinvention. For example, between 1985 and 2000, all the men's clothing stores, many of the women's clothing stores and a sporting goods store closed. These closures resulted in a forty percent vacancy rate. By 2000, however, fifteen new restaurants replaced the old retail, vacancy had dropped to ten percent and property values began to rise.

The time it took to begin to see the results of the reinvention was fifteen years. What if Mayor Campbell in his 1984 council meeting had said that his vision would take fifteen years? That would have been discouraging to most, if not all, who hoped for a reinvention. Once there is traction, as there was in Delray Beach, those watching the implementation schedule will forget about the time it is taking and celebrate the interim successes.

In the beginning stages of reinvention, there may be extreme pressure to show instant progress. The leader may be anxious to see action and may have made campaign promises he's trying to keep. The executive implementer has to maintain the schedule even if there's pressure to deviate from it. The implementation team must resist building a project for the sake of building a project, unless it contributes to the plan.

Delray Beach Redevelopment—
First Twelve Years

Date	Event
1984	» City Commission Meeting (1st Vision) » Establishment of the CRA
1985	» Committee Report (First Action Plan)
1987	» The First CRA Plan (no vision) » 1st Great Vision (Cultural Center)
1988	» 1st Executive Implementer
1989	» 1st Early Project: Streetscape of Mainstreet » 2nd Executive Implementer » City General Obligation Downtown Bond Issue
1990	» 3rd Executive Implementer » 1st Great Leader (Mayor) » Old School Square Cultural Center Redevelopment
1991	» 4th Executive Implementer (9 years) » 1st Core Team
1992	» 2nd CRA Plan by Executive Implementer » Implementation Start
1992–1996	» Executive Implementer's Full Team » Downtown Infrastructure Re-building
1996	» Redevelopment Traction (noticeable signs of change) » 12 Years for Visible Signs of Change

It took twelve years before redevelopment implementation became noticeable and people began saying: "I cannot believe what is happening to the downtown. Maybe the city can change." It took the ensuing years to produce a noticeable difference in physical appearance, reduction of crime, and rising taxable value:

Delray Beach Redevelopment— Visible Signs of Change

Date	Event
1990	» First street beautification (four blocks, mainstreet) » First cultural arts center (Old School Square)
1991	» Downtown brand ("Arts and Entertainment") » Fourth Executive Implementer » First mainstreet event (Art and Jazz on-the-Avenue)
1991–Present	» Major events on mainstreet
1992	» Community policing (innovative chief) » International Tennis Center (Virginia Slims)
1992–2008	» CRA business lending (restaurant emphasis)
1993	» First new restaurant (Elwood's) » Establishment of Central Marketing Management » First new housing project (Antilles) » First new coffee house (Java City)
1994	» 2 new restaurants (Chile Factory, Splendid Blendeds)
1994–1999	» Rebuilt municipal surface parking lots
1995	» Second mainstreet beautification (4 blocks)
1996	» First private sector retail redevelopment (Grove Sq.) » 3 New Restaurants
1996–2000	» 10 New Restaurants
1997	» First major addition to existing hotel (Marriott) » Pineapple Grove streetscape (2nd mainstreet) » Third mainstreet beautification (4 blocks) » New art gallery on mainstreet
1998	» 3rd downtown housing project (Mallory Sq)
1999	» New downtown restaurant (Dada)
2000	» Fourth downtown housing project (Atlantic Grove) » Fifth Executive Implementer (15 years)
2000–2015	» 38 new restaurants (mainstreet & secondary streets)
2001	» Second downtown housing project (Courtyards) » Third downtown housing project (Town Square)
2002	» Starbucks arrives on mainstreet

Delray Beach Redevelopment—
Visible Signs of Change, con't.

Date	Event
2003	» Fourth mainstreet beautification (6 blocks) » Fourth downtown housing project (Mallory Sq) » Fifth downtown housing project (Atlantic Grove) » Second hotel (Residence Inn, conversion) » Clean and Safe Program established (mainstreet)
2003–2015	» Health, beauty, fitness cluster (mainstreet, side streets)
2007	» Third new garage (213 Spaces, downtown)
2009	» Third new hotel (Seagate)
2011	» New mainstreet rental mixed-use housing project » Second arts center (Arts Garage)
2012–Present	» Four new downtown housing projects
2013	» Fourth new hotel (Hyatt Place)
2014	» First national clothing retailer on mainstreet (Urban Outfitters)
2015–Present	» Sixth Executive Implmenter » 3 national clothing retailers on mainstreet

Main Street store closing, 1990s. Delray Beach, Florida

Unfortunately, there may be times when the leader or others decide to stray from the vision and embrace an alternative or additional direction. This can be catastrophic to the schedule and can even result in failure of implementation. Forcefully refusing to modify the schedule for such distractions is necessary to avoid such an outcome.

6

PRIVATE INVESTMENT

So far, we have concentrated on the key actions that need to be taken by the public sector to improve the odds of success for reinventing targeted areas of a city. Step six of reinventing your city relates to engaging the private sector—the developers, investors, property owners, merchants, and other private sector partners.

We have discussed at length the role of the public sector and what should be considered as the public sector moves through a redevelopment process. The public sector cannot do it alone, however. The only way the public sector can truly redevelop an area is to get the private sector to participate. The private sector needs to be involved. In a big way. This actually is THE most difficult part of redevelopment, because no matter how good the vision, the leadership, the team, the plan and the implementation, if the private sector doesn't believe the area is worth investing its money, nothing will happen. Governments can't build their way to success; they can only create a platform for the private sector to build upon. The commercial buildings, the retail shops, the hotels, etc., will all be built by the private sector. They are the ones who will open and operate the shops, populate the office buildings and build the restaurants. They are the ones who will hire the employees. So there is a BIG delta between the public sector's investment and goals, and the private sector's interest in buying into those goals. This chapter will speak bluntly about what the private sector needs and wants before they will participate in the plan to reinvent your city.

This is also the stage where a reality check has to take place. We have gone into cities that are so blighted that no bank would even consider lending money to a check cashing store, let alone a national tenant, but national tenants were what the community and elected officials told us they wanted. "No," we told them."You are not going to get Old Navy or XYZ on blighted Main Street. Not now, not in the near future, and maybe never."

The City of West Palm Beach actually was in a position to attract Trader Joe's, the iconic, groupie-like food store. Raphael Clemente, the director of the Downtown Development Authority, came up with a fun and tantalizing marketing ploy to attract their attention. He asked stakeholders, visitors and the City: "What would you trade for a Trader Joe's?" City officials agreed to change the city's name to Trader Joe's for a day! He got the cameras rolling and went to a city commission meeting and had them all talk about Trader Joe's and renaming the city for a day. It was great! The city got good press and Trader Joe's acknowledged the clever campaign. Trader Joe's had very specific expansion plans and site selection criteria, and they didn't include West Palm Beach at that point in time. We don't doubt, however, that because of the innovative outreach the DDA and city did, Trader Joe's is likely to consider West Palm Beach in the future!

Expectations of the community as a whole, and sometimes even the elected officials, are often unrealistic and do not reflect what the private sector is willing to invest. A realistic assessment of what a city can expect from private investment and what the private sector is willing to do is required.

What type of private partner are you looking for? Big developers, medium-scale projects, or small mom and pops? This section covers all three scales of typical redevelopment patterns:

- Main Street
- Medium Scale
- Large Scale

Assuming the plan is written, or at least there has been sufficient discussion about how the city is going to reinvent itself, there should be some targets in terms of the private sector. Are you going to be Main Street with mom and pops? Do you have a major metropolis that can handle a million square feet of mixed-use, high-rise development, or is there a land assemblage that can be offered to attract development? It is important that the message and vision are clear, of course, and that you can target the right type of private investors, businesses or developers. Don't bother going after Old Navy if you know the demographics won't match their site criteria. Although each redevelopment area is unique and has to have its own set of issues and opportunities, there are some consistencies in how you set the stage for redevelopment to occur. The one common thread between the smallest mom and pop merchant and the largest developer is that they want to succeed and be profitable. If you understand what will make them profitable, you can put the right foundation in place to not only attract them to the city, but to help them flourish.

Main Street

Let's start with the smaller-scale main street environment. For the sake of defining that scale, we've applied some parameters for our main street real estate:

- Business Ownership—mom and pops, individual small retailers, small operators
- Land Ownership—single ownership of the buildings, or leased operations
- Average Investment to Rehabilitate—$10,000-$2 million (for a new restaurant)
- Square Footage—500 square feet to 8,000-10,000 square feet per unit

Let's assume the public sector has decided to lay the foundation for redevelopment to occur. It's in this planning phase that the city leaders should start to think about how they are going to get the private sector involved. Very often, there are only two types of private parties that are at the table in the beginning stages of redevelopment in a main street environment: 1) the ones that the city would like to relocate or remove because they themselves are part of the problem; and 2) the ones blocking redevelopment by holding onto property and not renovating or leasing to good tenants. Occasionally, there is a cluster of good tenants that you want to keep on main street, and who have patiently waited for the area to "turn around." The "new" or additional investors have yet to be found, and at this stage, they don't know what you're planning and probably have zero interest in finding out. How many times have we picked up the phone and called a restaurant operator we knew to tell them about a great new opportunity to open their second restaurant in a city we were working for? Responses usually range from belly laughter to some derogatory comments about the city we just mentioned. All too often, even experienced business owners and developers don't see the possibilities and opportunity in the beginning of an up and coming area.

So how do you begin to lay the foundation that the city is "on the upswing," "open for business" and "changing for the better"? It is hard, after all, to convince a successful restauranteur that the derelict, vacant street with boarded up storefronts will be a thriving entertainment area in the near future.

In general, there are two things that have to occur before the private sector will even contemplate opening a business or investing in your city. One, you must convince them (and everyone else) that at the very top of the chain (elected officials, city management, property owners) the commitment is there to redevelop the area. Two, you must convince them the negative environment (crime, trash, blight) is going to be addressed and the environment will be conducive to them succeeding in business. If it's clean and safe, you can get them to the table. If it's not, don't even approach them until you have a solid plan and can demonstrate how you're going to change the environment. Even if it's not clean and safe yet, as long as there is a plan, you can start to get folks involved in the process.

We like to draw up big pictures and plans of what we are planning to do, especially when there are major capital improvements planned, like streetscapes, open spaces, park upgrades, sidewalk improvements, trees or whatever. Then we host all kinds of events and activities to draw people to the area that wouldn't normally have come. For example, in Northwood Village in West Palm Beach, over 48 percent of the people initially surveyed thought Northwood Village was unsafe. After four years, the number dropped to 5 percent. How?

The street was a mess, the area was deemed unsafe, and there was a terrible tenant mix, with hardware stores, thrift shops and boarded-up buildings. The ones that were open were used for storage. Eventually, we found one tiny tenant who owned a pizza shop downtown about four miles from our redevelopment target area who was willing to take a risk (with some incentives from the city) and open a small restaurant. Once he went under construction, we rented the shop next door (for very little money) and let artists set up shop in there. Out of forty or so vacant blighted shops, two shops now had the desired mix of tenants that would create the vision for where the street was going. We held street fairs once a month and hosted an Art & Wine promenade. Our very talented marketing director, Sharon McCormick, lined the street with street vendors in front of the old shops to simulate what "could be" if people could envision nice shops there. Some of the street vendors sold food, but mostly they sold the illusion of activity that drew in people who would normally not visit the area. So what does that have to do with attracting private investment? Everything. It was during those events that suddenly the street was full of people. Through the lone restaurant under construction (which later opened), we were able to show other restaurants and merchants what the area could be like if it was populated with the right mix of merchants. It worked. Within three years, over 130 businesses opened—one shop at a time. Also, as we mentioned, occasionally there are a few existing merchants who are troupers and really want the area to turn around. Northwood had some gems with Rod Tinson, Steve Allred and Dave Romaine. They owned a series of antique stores on Main Street and became absolutely the best ambassadors the city could have had. They painted planter boxes and flower pots, they talked up what was happening, and they defended every positive step the city took to change the area. Those types of outspoken partners play a significant role and should be found early on and appreciated.

When we met with Charleston's Mayor Riley, he was in year thirty-nine of a forty-year term. We asked him about his first years in office. We knew that when he took the helm at the ripe old age of thirty-two, he had a handful of issues that he knew he needed to address if he was going to turn the downtown around—not the least of which was the crime rate and seemingly lawless atmosphere. "A lot of things had to happen, but people had to feel safe," he said. "We needed an excellent police chief and a good police force." He knew he had to change the image of the town being under siege, so he started by hiring a new chief of police, Reuben Greenberg, and began an era of zero tolerance for criminals.

Another memorable quote from our travels came from Mayor Riley. During our visit, he said, very matter of factly, "Police officers need to have a good relationship with the community. When they are loved by the community, the criminals are in trouble, because the community will rat out the bad guys. When they are NOT loved, the criminals have it a lot easier, because the community will not rat them out and will protect the bad guys. When the police are loved, the criminals are going to get caught!" How succinct is that for creating a platform for change?

If the community loves their police and assists them in crime prevention, there is an army of people fighting the crime wave, and the police have a solid basis on which to succeed. If the community is disengaged, or lackadaisical, about crime, the criminals have no real threat in the community. They can hang out easily among everyone else and not fear being turned in or pointed out as a target for the police.

Let's assume, then, that crime is being addressed or under control. What else can be done to attract private investment?

Promote the Future Before It Arrives

It's not a good idea to wait until the new streetscapes and roads are done, or the open spaces and parks are designed to start promoting the "new city." While the physical environment is being planned, the city should be promoting what WILL BE THERE, so business owners start to see the value in potentially opening a shop. Even if you have to stretch reality a bit in the interim.

Besides future merchants, the other target is investors and developers. If the area is positioned as up-and-coming, area investors will start to look for buildings to buy and renovate. The city should establish a system where potential investors can be taken into a "war room" that has maps and pictures and clearly shows the vision for the area. Prepare packages that have information on vacancies and rental rates, and comps on properties that have sold.

Attracting New Businesses

So where do you find these business owners?

They may be in the same city and want a second location. They may be in the next city over, or they may be far away. Remember the story about Oakland Park? A culinary arts district was branded in a city that had no main street, no downtown, and challenging demographics? Our marketing team videotaped a community meeting where they were presenting and telling everyone about what the city was going to become. They elaborated and showed slides about the vision and the types of businesses they were looking for. They talked about the culinary concept and the types of businesses that would be welcomed. The video was put on You Tube, and out of nowhere, they got a call from a brew pub that saw it. Within eighteen months, the owners opened an 18,000-square-foot operation!

That launched the culinary district! The marketing team may never have found that business on its own. It wasn't in the city, or the one next door, or the one next to that. The lesson here is to use social media and events when available to "sell your visions," and to position and promote what they will become. Look for trade organizations and trade shows. Join the International Council of Shopping Centers (ICSC) when looking for retailers. Join the Urban Land Institute (ULI) or the National Association of Industrial and Office Property (NAIOP) when looking for developers.

How do you convince them to join in your plan and spend money?

If you got past the first step and convinced them the area is going to be rehabilitated, then the next step is getting them to open a shop. A lot of this effort for smaller main street type tenants is about determining if they have the time and the capacity to expand. Someone running a restaurant doesn't have much time to spare, let alone leave the existing business, to run around trying to open a second location. There's usually an issue with raising funds to open the second business. Who's going to fund the new business startup expense?

There are a few things a city can do. If there are any funds available, use them to bring down the costs of opening the business, but consider putting those funds into the buildings themselves, not into the operation of the business. If the city invests in rehabbing a building and the business fails, at least the building will be renovated. The next business will not have that expense and will stand a better chance at success. Plus, you don't want to fund a point-of-sale machine and tables and chairs, only to have them walk out the door with the city's investment. If there are no funds available, consider using staff time to help them open. Provide them with business guidance, help them through the building department or permitting process, take them to the Chamber of Commerce for introductions to others who may be able to assist them. Introduce them to the banks and lenders in the community that you have forged relationships with. You need to form relationships with banks and other stakeholders so they will be there when you need them. Any form of support you can provide will only encourage and enable them to open their business. Once they open, help them with marketing. Hold street fairs, offer to do press releases, etc. In the beginning stages, any assistance and cheerleading you do for the businesses will only help to attract other new businesses. Package your story in an attractive way and make sure everyone is "selling" the same vision. Give talks to area homeowner groups and teach the merchants how to sell the new vision. Make sure everyone has the right contact info, and that there is one source to go to when businesses start inquiring about investing.

What if your targeted businesses don't want to open a business?

Keep trying.

One time, we chased after a restaurant owner for four years. Finally, the timing was right, and the restaurant decided to take the chance and open. There really is no magic bullet or formula. It's just daily outreach and pounding the pavement and not giving up. It takes time and a lot of effort, but it pays off if you keep at it. And don't get deterred by people or critics who supposedly know better when they still see vacancies after a year of you trying to change the street or area. Tell them the stores will open over time, and they will if you keep trying and do all the other things we've talked about.

Medium-Scale Developments

These types of projects are quite different from main street businesses, and the approach to attract them is quite different. Again, for scale, we've applied these parameters:

- Company Ownership—sophisticated builders, developers
- Land Ownership—private sector land owner, developer, builder (maybe the city owns parcels)
- Average Investment—$1 million–$20 million
- Square Footage—1,000–25,000 square feet of retail, 25–150 units, 1,000–40,000 square feet office

Avenue Lofts. Fort Lauderdale, Florida

These types of projects are market-driven. Developers of medium-scaled, mixed-use projects are always on the lookout for land and development opportunities. They will gravitate to areas with limited risk, and that have other buildings like the ones they build already in place, and with an active real estate market. Well, if your city had that situation, there wouldn't be an issue, would there? But this is about cities who are trying to change market conditions and convince developers to see the vision and take a risk!

Realize that at this scale of development, you not only have to convince the builder or developer to invest in your city, you'll have to get the lenders or financiers convinced, too, which often is more difficult.

So what has to happen to create a market for the private sector to build a mixed-use project or a medium-sized development in your city?

The very first thing that must happen, as outlined in Chapter One, is the developers and the lenders have to be able to see, and then buy into, the vision you created. If done correctly, they will be able to calculate the level of risk they are taking until the area catches up with their investment. Just as important, as stated in Chapters Two, Three and Four, the leadership, the team and the plan all have to be in place well in advance. Without those supporting elements in place, the vision alone will not convince anyone to risk $20 million. So, let's assume all of those elements are in place.

Now it boils down to the market. Who owns the land where the development may occur? If it's the public sector, the game just got easier, because the ability to partner with the developer and create a land value formula that makes financial sense is within reach. Some cities are comfortable with this type of public-private partnership, while others are not. If a city owns land and is not willing to use the value of the land to stabilize a real estate project, then they should sell the land. In that case, the city is the one blocking development. Unless a city is extremely skilled in strategic land acquisition that will yield future value, a city should not buy and hold land, then try to sell it at "market rates" in a distressed or redevelopment area. That's another way of holding up the private sector real estate market.

We have seen some cities that take a great deal of time to acquire and assemble land under the guise of redeveloping it one day, then they sit and sit and sit on it for years. They can't figure out why no one wants to develop it. It's likely due to a lack of vision and leadership, but it could also be because: a) their expectations related to leasing or selling it are not realistic; or b) they don't know, or can't agree on, what they want to use it for.

Tim Hernandez, a developer in South Florida, is very keen on spotting redevelopment areas that have potential, and he is easily enticed to look at the opportunities and options for development. That said, he is very careful in his assessment of what the risk factors are.

Tim said that when he's assessing an area, he looks for places where people want to live! "In most cases, where there was opportunity, change was happening. There was some form of public investment going on so we found opportunity. If there is an opportunity to create residential that can support the retail, we can create an urban environment that wasn't there before."

Another point he made is that, "Real estate is a reactive business—someone always copies the first guy. The goal is to identify an imbalance in supply and demand." Tim's team saw demand for housing near activity. "In mixed communities where yuppies, empty nesters, etc. live and work nearby each other, there is usually an opportunity to provide more housing and retail because those uses feed off each other."

Tim also emphasized that the private sector usually can't create a new environment from scratch. "To create from scratch was too hard, but in Delray Beach, Florida, they (they being the city redevelopment folks) had started it, so we leveraged public activity. Private sector won't be able to create it all."

The developers are also paying close attention to assessing the area to see if the project will work. They look at crime, proximity to schools, pricing variations, etc.

The financial markets are also of huge importance to mid-sized redevelopment projects. Since 2008, equity requirements have changed, and this has reduced the size of projects because lenders don't like the exposure a large project brings. This is changing, but in the meantime, there is no getting around the new conditions developers face when trying to finance projects since the "Great Recession."

Sometimes the private sector can be a problem if they also are just sitting on land. If the private sector owns the land, it becomes more difficult if the property owners are not sufficiently interested in your plan to redevelop an area. You can't force someone to sell their land, unless your state has maintained eminent domain powers. By virtue of the landmark Supreme Court eminent domain case, *Kelo vs. City of New London, Connecticut*, decided in 2005, most states now limit what government can do in terms of taking land for private development. *For the record, we believe that with the appropriate protections in place, eminent domain has a place in government for redevelopment purposes.* But without getting into the pros and cons of eminent domain at this point, let's assume it's not an option.

Privately held land can be targeted for redevelopment the same way that public land can in the sense of the vision and plans for the area. If property owners are approached and brought into the fold early on, they may see the value you are creating by putting the forces in place to increase the value of their land. If they see the momentum and the leadership driving to improve the area, they may participate and begin to look for ways to capitalize on your efforts. Some cities have the ability to provide tax incentives or tax rebates on land development deals. Those can be very helpful if the area suffers from poor market conditions. A simple tax rebate can make the difference in the lender being willing to finance the project or not. In some cases, if there is a redevelopment arm of the city or county, or an economic development arm, they can provide guarantees to the loans. In cases where there are no incentives, a city may look for state or federal grants, or assist in the public portion of the redevelopment, such as underground utilities upgrades, or above-ground streetscapes, or even the relocation of utilities. All those public investments reduce the cost to the private developer that make financing the deal easier.

On more than one occasion, we have gone with a builder or developer to the lender, and sat together to demonstrate the commitment of the public sector to support the private developer's project. That show of solidarity can go a long way in providing the lender comfort that the city is leading and committed to reinventing the area.

Tim Hernandez noted that "as a middle-sized guy, we don't have resources like a public company to compete and be successful. It takes the same process to develop a thirty-unit project as a 300-unit one, so cities need to help small and middle-sized guys wherever possible. If you are waiting for a public company to come in, you will wait a long time (from the beginning stages of redevelopment)."

That is a really good point, because some cities think that they should assemble a lot of land, and/or hold out until a large-scale redevelopment project takes place. There are multiple issues with that strategy, but it's certainly not one that will likely work, primarily due to market conditions. A better strategy is, instead of waiting for a large, publically traded development company to come in as a silver bullet and redevelop the town, to start with the smaller, doable projects, and show tangible evidence of progress. The bigger guys will come later.

ELECTED OFFICIALS SHOULD STOP READING HERE AND GO TO THE NEXT CHAPTER

Before we get to the large-scale development discussion, note that both midsized and large-scale developers have one thing in common: they count votes.

Tim Hernandez lamented about one project he wished he would have passed on because he got caught up in the dysfunctional politics of the town. "If there is consistently 4-1 or 5-0 votes, you can correlate that to successful redevelopment. If there are 3-2 votes, the progress is slow," he said.

BAM! How telling is that!

It's true, though. If we are going to be honest here, we need to admit that watching elected officials squabble over every little agenda item to the exasperation of everyone else is painful to watch. Plus, as Tim said, it usually translates into dysfunction when they start talking about approving a project or not. We're not talking about the important issues that need a great deal of debate and a good, often heated discussion. We're talking about the kind of elected body where almost every decision has some divisiveness to it, due to simple politics, and there is no real leadership to keep the discussion from derailing. "As a developer, we need to know the city is there to help us and put their money where their mouth is," Tim said. "That means they need to be fairly aligned with the vision and continuously make decisions that move in that direction."

In closing, Tim said developers of his ilk look for an intersection of three important factors:

1. Regulatory and environmental conditions conducive to redevelopment
2. Good market conditions and forces
3. Transaction structure or financial terms that work

Clearly, the cities have total control over the first factor by drafting land use and zoning codes that promote redevelopment, but they can also impact the other two, as discussed in Chapter Seven: Financing Redevelopment.

Large-Scale Developments

- Ownership—REITS, highly sophisticated builders, developers
- Average Investment—$20 million-$350 million or more
- Square Footage—10,000-750,000 square feet of retail, 100-2000 units, 50,000-400,000 square feet office

What is a true public/private partnership?

The term "public/private partnership" is used a lot these days. In general, there are two types. The first is where the private sector agrees to build a public facility, like a highway or a public building, then charges a user fee or bills the government to repay the debt on the asset. The second type relates to real estate or land deals. Those public/private partnerships usually involve a real estate deal where the private sector is going to build something, and the public sector is going to participate in a substantive way, either through land contribution, financing, or another public form of investment in the project. We are going to talk about the real estate type of a public/private partnership.

Starting in the late 1990s, when downtown revitalization kicked into high gear and cities started to realize they needed to stop spreading out to the suburbs and reinvest in their downtowns, one of our country's largest public/private partnerships at the time was about to begin. As previously discussed, it's called CityPlace, a large, mixed-use development in West Palm Beach, Florida.

In Chapter Two, and again in the case study section, we talk about CityPlace from the public sector's vantage point. Let's review how the private sector viewed that investment.

High-rise residential building. Sarasota, Florida

CityPlace office tower. West Palm Beach, Florida

CityPlace Development:

Total Acres	72
Retail	600,000 sq. ft.
Residential Units	420
Commercial	350,000 sq. ft.
Hotel	400 rooms
Parking Garages	3500 spaces

What made the private sector, Related Urban, willing to invest in such a large scale, high-risk venture?

Kenneth A. Himmel is president and chief executive officer of Related Urban, which according to their web site, is *"the nation's leading developer of large-scale mixed-use properties."* Related Urban, formed in 1997, is the mixed-use development division of Related Companies. Per their website;

> *"Under Mr. Himmel's leadership, Related Urban has opened two award-winning iconic destinations—Time Warner Center in New York City and CityPlace in West Palm Beach. Both of these projects have created a significant impact in the growth and transformation of their respective surrounding urban core. 'Time Warner Center was like climbing the mountain of mountains. The way we executed it and the way it has become a part of the city and a catalyst for the West Side of New York speaks very well of the work we did. We really pulled off something pretty special,'" said Himmel.*

Large-scale developments like CityPlace are rare and require a great deal of expertise, financial capacity and time. The assemblage alone can take a decade or more. They are also usually reserved for larger cities where there is enough density to ensure the project is sustainable.

CityPlace was built in 2000, and we've had the opportunity to watch Ken and his team at Related successfully and skillfully manage the CityPlace property over the last decade, which included a very difficult real estate recession.

Management is just one of the very important traits a city should look for in a private sector partner when entering into a public-private partnership. It's one thing to find a qualified developer. It's quite another to find one that can handle the ups and downs of the real estate market, and continue to protect not only the real estate asset, but the integrity of the downtown at the same time.

Ken told us what he and business partner Steve Ross saw that intrigued them to respond to the bid to develop the 72-acre parcel in a relatively small city. "There was growth opportunity, there was a large assemblage, the city was behind the project, the path was clear on how the city would help the process along the way, the location was great (being across from the wealthy enclave of Palm Beach), the site was not far from the airport, and we had confidence in the mayor at the time, Nancy Graham." This basically sums up what we have spent the last six chapters talking about, and the important roles the public sector must play. This particular public/private partnership may be one of the best examples of "how to" in the country, considering the city is on amendment #19 to the development agreement, and the partnership is still intact. And, significantly, Graham and her team negotiated a deal that did not put the city at any financial risk.

We also asked Ken what the public sector should consider when they enter into these types of public-private deals and he was quick to respond "that one of the most important aspects of the deal is to ensure the public sector understands the economics of the deal so everyone wins." This is not easily accomplished, because seldom does a city have the real estate expertise in-house to sit across the table from the likes of a Related Company. Sometimes (unfortunately) a city is too afraid, cheap or proud to admit they don't have the expertise and they try going it alone with in-house staff. Very often, those deals fall apart because the city may be so averse to making a bad deal that they are overly conservative and they try to play hard ball, only to run the developer off. Even in West Palm Beach, where Mayor Graham was an attorney and clearly an intelligent and analytical individual who studied mixed-use projects at length, she still sought outside expertise to form the right team to negotiate the deal.

Two essential areas of industry expertise Ken noted are important to making these types of deals work are economic development consulting firms and pro-business law firms. "A city needs people at the table who understand the economics of the deal, but who also understand the other positives that projects bring to the city, including employment, tax revenue, quality of life, and the overall halo effect of growth, as opposed to trying to squeeze every last dime out of the developer." Related prides themselves on setting a higher quality standard, and Ken emphasized the need for quality partners, including also, architects and planners.

Assembling Land

Other large-scale projects can be achieved in smaller towns, and a city should absolutely take the time to assemble land if they see the potential—even if it takes a decade or more. In Pompano Beach, the redevelopment agency started acquiring land in the '90s at the major intersection and exit ramp off of the busy Interstate 95. It took until 2014 before the last key parcel was purchased to enable a new, high-density commerce park concept to reach the point where a bid could go out looking for developers. A commerce park with office, hotel and residential uses is now envisioned around a large retention area, creating a nice pedestrian promenade. The jobs that will be created for the city, including the blighted areas surrounding the park, are going to have a major impact on the city's workforce. It took almost twenty years of preparation. In the meantime, the land use amendment was done, the zoning was modified, the overall vision for the surrounding area was created, the main street and entertainment area got new streetscapes and started to revitalize, and the general climate for private investment in the city went from frigid to red hot. It's now apparent that, even though it took almost twenty years to assemble the land, the payoff will indeed be huge.

Collecting data for these types of projects is also a good idea so the public sector can share the market potential with developers and investors.

Transit Corridor and Office Park site. Pompano Beach, Florida

Be careful of data, however—it can be quite deceiving, and can be misused or interpreted incorrectly. For example, almost all of the data collected during the twenty years of assembling the land in the last example was quite useless at the point in time that the final piece was acquired. Real estate markets change so fast, and there are so many considerations, it really does not matter what the data indicated twenty, fifteen, ten, or even five years ago. In fact, one economist did a study centered on this 40-acre parcel and stated that the surrounding four corners should be redeveloped into commercial uses, and that there was tremendous potential for the area. While the economist's view was probably accurate for the long term, should the city wait until the other 120 acres were assembled before they issued a bid on the first 40 acres? Of course not! The market will change after the first 40 acres are developed, which would require an updated report, which in turn would reflect the new economic conditions of the area. Another danger is getting too ambitious. While 40 acres isn't the largest development in the world, don't wait until an entire area is assembled to start projects.

It may never get started. Conversely, don't chop a targeted assembly into tiny, useless pieces either.

One obstacle to large-scale development is insufficient utilities. Inevitably, the infrastructure is inadequate to support a new, large-scale development. One of the best pre-development efforts a city can undertake to prepare for the private sector's entry to the city is investment in infrastructure. Also figuring out where the land skeletons are is very helpful. It's a really "bad thing" when all the land is assembled and the bids have gone out, and everyone is excited about a pending development, only to find out spotted owls or an ancient Indian burial ground were there first.

The larger the development, the more important timing and city cooperation are. Developers need to know where they stand and have certainty to take to the bank—literally. That was one of the first things Ken Himmel said about West Palm Beach's CityPlace that resulted in his firm's interest in bidding on the project—the timing of the project and the cooperation of the city was key.

For these large projects, everything from land value to zoning regulations can make or break the deal. One of the most valuable tools a city has is a land markdown if they own the land. If not, they can assist in providing infrastructure and other city utilities to support the development. This assumes the project won't pencil out on its own because it's in a semi-blighted or transitional area that doesn't have a strong enough market to financially support itself.

Many states have some form of tax increment financing and that's a very powerful tool for financing large-scale projects. The new taxes generated from a project fund some part of the project, or collectively, an area. Enterprise zones, urban infill areas, state and federal grant and other tools should all be reviewed for large projects at the beginning stages.

It's amazing how from the smallest project (an ice cream store opening), to the largest development (of a mixed-use building), the involvement of the private sector and the activity it brings is the part of redevelopment that usually stirs the community's soul the most. It's the most visible aspect of all because the land takes on a new dimension when a small business opens, or a large development breaks ground. And everyone, especially elected officials, loves groundbreakings!

Remember,
> "The road to success is always under construction."
> —Lily Tomlin

7

FINANCING REDEVELOPMENT

We could write an entire book on the seventh step—financing the plan. Each and every city "reinvention" needs its own personalized finance plan. Without exception, there must be some sort of coherent financial strategy in place, because the absence of a workable finance plan will doom any effort no matter how well planned otherwise.

The starting point is based on one of two scenarios: either the city, or some branch of the city, has a funding source to draw from; or, there is absolutely no existing funding source and one has to be found. We will work through both scenarios.

No Funding Source in Place

Some cities go right to the planning stage and create big lofty goals without considering how they will pay for the recommendations in the plan. In general, it is always better to try to determine how much funding you can realistically access over a three-to-five-year period and then leverage as much of that funding as possible to have the biggest impact. We always start with the money and work our way backwards into what projects we can afford. Once you know how much money you have for projects, you draft a finance plan that includes all the potential sources of funds and all the potential uses or expenditures you intend to make. In a five-year plan, everyone can clearly see where the funding is coming from and what you intend to spend it on.

These types of finance plans are very powerful because they give the private sector a long-term view of how much money will be invested in an area, or what funds, if any, are available to support an area's revitalization goals.

While some plans are needed to guide zoning and urban design decisions, simply having a corridor plan, a downtown plan, or a master plan, is usually a waste of money unless it has a financial component. An exception to that is if you know you plan on doing streetscapes and other capital projects on state or federal roads, and are going to apply for state or federal grants. Some cities and counties write up long lists of objectives to fix blighted areas, seek affordable housing, or list job creation goals. All of that is great, but if you don't have a financial plan, nothing will happen. One county in south Florida has a redevelopment program and a plan with pages and pages of goals and objectives, but the county never funded the program. Care to speculate on how that's going?

A much better approach is to step back and envision how an area will transform itself. Next, determine what the public sector has to do to attract the private sector to come and invest. Then work towards determining how much money you will need.

It is at this early stage that a realistic approach is defined. For example, if it's going to take a $5 million streetscape with parking and lighting to sufficiently transform an area for retailers to come, having $500,000 isn't going to cut it. Change your strategy to fit your budget. So, if a $5 million streetscape is indeed needed, and it can be done in phases, don't change the goal. Match the phasing of your projects to the funding you have. Start with one retailer and one area, but have a longer term plan showing how over time you will get the $5 million. If there is no hope and there is no path to get the $5 million, start with the $500,000 anyway and put "to be determined" (TBD) in the finance plan. At a minimum, it shows you know where you want to go and are looking for the funding to get there.

If the goal is to attract new retail or commercial, but the demographics are not there to support that goal, you will need to prepare a financing strategy to deal with the demographic gap. One such strategy could be to provide incentives to attract new residential BEFORE you build a streetscape for the retail.

Similarly, if the goal is to attract new retail or commercial and the demographics *are* sufficient to support it, you will need to precisely identify why the retailers aren't coming to town and align your finance plan to attract them. Perhaps they need assistance with facade improvements. Perhaps they need more assistance with the interior build-out of their restaurants. Perhaps there is no parking, or it's dimly lit. Perhaps they simply don't know what your plans are for the area and you need to do a marketing campaign. All of the solutions must be translated into a quantifiable dollar amount and put into a finance plan.

Please note that if you're wrong about the goal and the solution, having the finance plan won't be of much help. However, if you write a workable plan and know what you need to do, you then have to finance the pieces that will instantly attract the private sector.

Starting a redevelopment program with little or no funding is like starting off after college with no money. After college, you typically don't have any money for a down payment on a house that will build equity. New college graduates may not make a big salary, so there are limited options to save or invest. A city with no funding sources needs to think of itself as a college student who *must* find even a small amount of money each month to put away in a savings account or to invest. Even if a city can only find a few thousand dollars to promote its goals, and puts those goals in a finance plan, the road to investment will begin. One funding strategy is to capture new money that comes in from the investment that was made. For example, if $10,000 is set aside to attract and open new businesses, some of the money from the new businesses can go back into a fund. The new money can come from the increased taxes generated, business tax receipts, or from other fees. Whatever the source is, it needs to be a consistent formula that can be counted on for reinvestment.

What starts to happen over time in a redevelopment area is a spin-off effect that is usually measurable. If businesses start to open, the residential neighborhoods nearby become more attractive and the housing stabilizes or values start to go up. Some of the increase in the city's economic wealth needs to be set aside for "investment." That investment needs to be identified in a finance plan so everyone can see from year to year where that future investment will take place.

One city we worked in was determined to only do public-type investments. They were focused only on constructing a city hall and keeping their vacant parcels for a future park. The problem with that strategy is there is no leverage; simply building a city hall won't attract the private sector to invest. In this case, there is no new private investment. The city doesn't build their tax base; yet, they still have to fund the new city hall, pay for and maintain the park. If part of the financing strategy was instead to build a city hall, sell the vacant land (and use the money to build a park elsewhere), then use the new taxes generated from the new project to pay to maintain the park, they would create a self-funding situation from just one new private project. Some of the city's money should always go toward attracting private and/or business development.

What if there is a long stretch of a tired and blighted corridor and your commissioners or city council says, "We need to do something on that corridor!" So, you hire a consultant who draws pretty pictures of people strolling down the corridor. Then what? Don't do a corridor plan without being very sure how you are going to engage the private sector to join you. Ask what you as the public sector have to spend to get the businesses to change, or open, or build? Do they need incentives? Do they need utility work to make their project work? Do they need the zoning changed? Is the area safe, or do you need to add security, etc.?

Funding Options

A few general options for redevelopment funding may include the following:

Tax Increment Financing: A TIF program captures funds from new projects and reinvests them back into a specific geographic area. The entity is referred to as a community redevelopment agency (CRA), a taxing district (TAD), a redevelopment district (RAD), or other acronyms throughout the country with a similar formula. This is one of the most effective tools a state can allow because it provides an ongoing dedicated source of revenue that can be leveraged and used to issue large bonds. In the state of Florida, some counties have begun to fight against these funding tools because they want to keep the share of the county tax money that currently flows into a municipal CRA. Board members of these entities can either be elected officials or outside appointed members, or a combination of the two, depending on the state and the statute that governs them.

> *Mayor Riley from Charleston and his staff used this tool for many of the successful projects that turned that downtown around. The city and the county both understood that investing in an area for an extended period of time is the most effective way to reinvent a city or an area. In our discussion, one of Riley's staff members was mortified to hear that some Florida counties would be so shortsighted as to limit their investment in an attempt to capture the funds for themselves, or to limit or stop these funding mechanisms.*

Downtown Development Authorities: A DDA is a special taxing district that uses a formula to tax property owners in a specific geographic area. DDA's are limited in the amount of tax they can charge, but if the area is large enough and the property values are high enough, the amount of money for redevelopment efforts can be quite significant. DDA's can only be created by state legislation in most states.

Business Improvement Districts (BID): These districts are most often used when the property owners agree to tax themselves based on a formula and use the funds to improve the business district. There is no state oversight or involvement and it's a more localized type of special taxing initiative. BIDS, unlike DDA's, usually limit their funds to marketing, security, etc., whereas CRA's and DDA's tend to invest in capital-intense projects, such as streetscapes, garages, etc.

Grants: Most states and, of course, the federal government, have various types of grants that a city or entity can apply for ranging from roadway improvements, waterway investment like docks and ramps, environmental grants, parks and open space grants, and many more.

Income-Producing Opportunities: Some cities have redevelopment operations that generate funds from programming. Those can range from small loan programs, rentals on buildings or businesses, renting open venues, etc.

Parking Funds: As previously discussed, one of the most valuable tools to meet parking needs in a growing city is a parking enterprise fund. That's simply the collection of parking revenue into a dedicated fund that can be leveraged to issue debt to build more parking. Cities that don't manage their parking effectively are losing out on a substantial amount of revenue that can be used to promote redevelopment efforts downtown, in business districts, and anywhere there are public parking venues.

Real Estate: Unfortunately, cities generally do not manage their real estate assets very well. Often they own a substantial amount of real estate assets and may even act as landlords. In many cases, they have acquired vacant lots for free from tax deed sales, or transfers from the county. The largest cities sometimes own the most valuable real estate in town. Where City Hall itself is located is often valuable property. One of the places a city can look for funds is in its real estate holdings. Can a city sell some property to generate funds? Can City Hall be moved to a less valuable location when it's reached its useful lifespan? Are city leases being monitored and do they reflect current market rates? We continuously help cities work through these issues and often act as their real estate asset management department. Some cities are shocked at how much money they have been losing!

Enterprise Funds: Some states have enterprise funds that vary in usage. These funds are usually reserved for state applications, or to meet state guidelines, such as a tax rebate on construction materials.

Existing or Targeted Funding Sources

Let's assume that the city has cobbled together enough money to either write a plan or has hired someone specialized in this field, to create an overall vision for what should happen next. Let's also assume that the plan that was written is a redevelopment implementation plan, not a zoning, urban design, corridor study, downtown, or master plan. Remember, in Chapter Four we said those plans alone won't work to reinvent a city.

The first step is to determine the highest and best use of the existing funds to leverage private investment to get more funds. One city client of ours has $12 million in the bank and a whole lot of land they assembled over the past decade. The emphasis and focus should be on getting that vacant land developed. For years, the city has had many fits and starts on those parcels mainly because they didn't have the right approach to attract the private sector. We are currently in the middle of proposing a very specific type of real estate transaction that will concentrate on leveraging the private sector's investment to fund improvements that will not only result in that parcel being developed, but will act as a catalyst for other surrounding development to occur. It will all be very clearly spelled out in a finance plan, not a master plan, or urban design plan. This city has paid for many of those "plans," and like many other cities in the same situation, it was falsely led to believe that design drives development. *Real estate drives development.*

City visionaries have to switch their thinking away from solely planning and design, and start by thinking about how to finance redevelopment. It works every time. If a city is fortunate enough to have a funding source, it should be allocated over a five-year period to show where the investment will go and how much new revenue will be leveraged as a result of the public investment. The first step will be making sure the finance plan funnels the funds it has into the community in such a way that the tide turns immediately from a city with little or no redevelopment activity to a hot area.

Nothing promotes interest in the development community more than a city that invests in itself.

By no measure is this an exhaustive list of funding options; rather, it is a brief overview of some of the obvious and most often used tools. If there is no dedicated source of funding available, the city must create its own sources and match the dedicated annual allotment to specific expenditures tied to the redevelopment plan. Even if the city doesn't have any of the special agencies noted above, the concept can still be achieved with strategic use of general funds.

8

REINVENTING THE CITY

Introduction

After your reinvention is declared a success, it's time to sit down at a sidewalk café and celebrate—drinking an espresso at Starbucks in the morning or sipping a burgundy at a French bistro in the early evening. How long should you sit and enjoy the fruits of the labor of leaders, executive implementers, and highly effective team members? How long should you celebrate the many new residents, new and unique retailers lining beautified streets, and countless activities at cultural facilities constructed over the years? How long? The answer is, "Pay the bill and get back to work. You have more to do."

Pause and Get a Check Up

At the end of the initial reinvention cycle, the leader and the executive implementer should pause for a few minutes (really months) and take a look the plan. The documents used in the first reinventing of your city will serve as a checklist for beginning the next cycle of reinvention. These documents include the original, or the latest statement of the vision, the plan itself, the implementation strategy, and the list of unfinished, unfunded and incomplete projects. A financial analysis of the work performed during the initial reinvention should be performed. What projects contributed to property values and tax growth, and where were those projects located geographically?

What projects did not experience increases in value and where were they located?

Should the less developed or less successful reinvention areas be the next target areas? Should an area that produced little return on investment still be considered? These are the types of questions that should be asked during this reinvention checkup.

Once an objective assessment of the initial reinvention is completed, it is time to create the vision for reinventing your city in its next cycle. After a successful implementation has occurred over a period of as long as twenty five years, much will have changed. The leader will want to invite all who are interested to participate in creating the new vision.

After a new vision has been conceived, it is, of course, time to make a plan that supports the vision. During the checkup, it will be useful to look at the current plan or sets of plans, determine the areas of progress over the past two decades or so, and to evaluate what was implemented and what was not. It may be possible during this cycle to update the original plan, rather than start with a completely new document.

Team evaluation is also required. Do you have the same executive implementer? Has your core team changed? Are they up for the new vision, a change of course, new projects, a new play book? Or are they tired, lacking energy? Should they be replaced? Assembling the right team is no less critical as you begin the next reinvention of your city.

The remaining steps—implementing the plan, engaging the private sector, and financing the plan, require the same attention that was given during the initial reinvention. The one significant difference is that, for this reinvention, if you followed the steps to reinventing your city initially, the process will be much more familiar and will benefit from the assessment of the first reinvention.

Below are some observations and examples of what you will discover after you have successfully completed the first reinventing of your city.

Fresh New Ideas

As part of reinventing, there is an ongoing need to initiate new ideas; ideas that resonate with new residents and visitors to the city. New ideas come from all members of the implementation team, as well as from outside contributors. Fresh marketing ideas may include new ways to position the city's brand. Such ideas may involve changed imagery, tag lines, logos, graphics, signs, and streetscapes. Programming and changed demographics should be considered for the city's cultural facilities. For example, this type of assessment was conducted for The New World Symphony in the City of Miami Beach. As a result, the architecture changed. A new theater was developed. Marketing and programming became geared to Miami Beach's younger demographics.

New World Symphony. Miami Beach, Florida

First Fix the Little Things

Often, when implementation is considered complete for the initial reinvention, there are still some projects that, for a variety of reasons, were simply not finished. Identifying those unfinished projects that can be completed during the early stages of the next cycle of reinvention is a useful exercise. Additionally, there may be issues that arise as unintended consequences of the reinvention success. These unintended consequences often result from the influx of so many restaurants and new business to an area and the increase in pedestrian and vehicular traffic. As we have seen, Delray Beach has enjoyed a very successful reinvention. Its success, however, has not been without some consequences. Here is a list of some issues that need to be addressed:

- Office uses such as law firms occupying ground floor space intended for retail;
- Odors caused by garbage accumulating in the rear of multiple restaurants;
- Litter, such as gum sticking to the sidewalk and cigarette butts;
- Traffic congestion increasing on main street;
- Lack of adequate parking and parking meters;
- Encroachment by restaurants' outdoor cafes into the pedestrian passageway resulting in too narrow sidewalks;
- Insufficient dog parks and dog watering facilities;
- Lack of a central plaza to attract residents and visitors to relax and play;
- Insufficient urban parks;
- Increased maintenance required for downtown;
- Barkers, employed by restaurants to attract customers walking by, have become disruptive;

What's Missing in the Urban City?

Ana Novak, who you met in the Introduction, is now an expert urban dweller, having lived in Delray Beach for three years. Like Ana, every urban dweller in a successful urban city becomes an urban expert. What a change it will be to have vision meetings with so many new urban experts in 2015, compared to those who attended such meetings in 1990. Some of the vision may be the same, such as "a safe and clean city," but suggestions by expert urban dwellers may include "We need more urban parks for dogs and people," or "There is too much traffic downtown," or "Let's manage downtown parking so that residents have a chance to eat out instead of employees working in." There are many examples of successfully reinvented cities that need both little and big improvements. Demographics change and cities respond to those changes. In San Francisco, high-tech companies are moving to the city from Silicon Valley. With the influx of these companies, young, talented professionals are moving to the city too. They eat everything from peanut butter to tenderloin and drink everything from cold pressed kale juice to white Bordeaux. Food in San Francisco is being reinvented as well. The next Alice Waters will emerge and we may read about her soon.

As we have seen, Bilbao is a great example of reinventing a city. It, too, still has things missing, including more knowledge-based industries, more workforce housing, more restaurants, more coffee houses, more small urban parks, more recreational opportunities, younger residents, and a "SoHo" type district. Bilbao's second twenty-five years may be the most important years of its reinvention, if leaders there follow Metropoli-30's recommendation to make the city the world center of science and technology by expanding its institutions. Like Oakland Park, Bilbao can reimagine itself as a culinary center. Along with colleges of science and technology, a culinary college could be considered. And, Bilbao can build on its reputation of having Michelin-starred restaurants by focusing on attracting new diverse and high quality restaurants to supports its "culinary" brand.

Watch for Competition from Other Cities

During the reinvention of your city, bear in mind that other cities are watching your success. Your competition will copy you and some may be successful. To stay ahead of the competition, you need to be vigilant about working on fresh and creative ideas for your city. Reinvention must be done daily, not every twenty-five years. It is not unlike the store windows on Fifth Avenue in New York City, which may change every month, every week and even every day. Without such vigilance, your town may become stale and, perhaps, even worse, boring.

Market Changes

After twenty-five years of reinventing a city, including a successful downtown and its adjoining neighborhoods, the market will have changed dramatically. Delray Beach in 1990 was a tired city, occupied by retirees or the nearly-retired. Today in 2015, the single-family residential neighborhoods surrounding the downtown are full of families with children, empty nesters, and active retirees. There are no nursing homes in downtown Delray Beach. The downtown residents are represented by millennials and young professionals. The median age of Delray Beach has dropped from fifty-five to forty-six. In twenty five years. This demographic change is typical for many successful urban cities.

A successfully reinvented downtown sees a change in retailing almost simultaneously with the advent of downtown apartments. Office demand may lag, but offices do eventually appear as CEOs of small and medium-sized businesses move their residence to a "hip" urban city. And eventually, they move their business headquarters, as well, particularly after they get tired of driving from their lovable urban core to the dreaded suburban office park. And why not? For lunch, employees can walk to a boutique restaurant or meet with colleagues for wine and cheese after work. Social life occurs all day in an exciting urban city. The drive home is five minutes, not fifty-five minutes, or the walk home is three minutes. Often reinvention will signal the need for a strong policy to attract developers to build Class A office space for the successful executives who live in the same city, so that office use is not limited to just small and medium sized businesses. Medium-sized box stores are not known to favor building in the urban downtowns (except in New York City or Chicago). However, in Delray Beach in 2013 and 2014, two major national food retailers, Fresh Market Grocery Store and Trader Joe's, each about 17,000 square feet in size, moved to the edge of downtown about ten blocks from the downtown core. Why? Delray Beach's demographics changed, and the grocery stores' customers are now living downtown and in the near-downtown's older neighborhoods. Notably, the two food stores still located to a suburban-style setting where surface parking is ample. In the future, those stores and others will locate in the heart of a downtown in order to be even closer to their customers who will want to walk rather than drive.

Traffic Problems

In many instances, an unintended consequence of successful reinvention is traffic, traffic and more traffic. Pedestrian traffic, the kind of traffic found on downtown sidewalks and reinvented neighborhoods is part of the reason reinvention is considered successful. People sit at outdoor cafés not just for dinner, but to look at the people traffic too. And for those of us who "people watch," people are pretty interesting; they come in all sizes, shapes and colors and are often much like art. Automobile traffic is a different experience entirely. It is caused by people driving from the suburbs or neighboring cities looking for a place to park so they can enjoy a delicious dinner at a restaurant or sidewalk café. The problem may not be the automobile or the customer driving, it may be (and often is) poor street design and poor parking management by the city. What is the solution? More parking lots, more signage directing people to those lots, electronic signs that tell you how many spaces are available in a particular area, flexible meter rates that charge more per hour for really convenient parking and less for garages located a block or two away from the main street.

The City of West Palm Beach is dealing with its traffic issues. The city instituted two very important traffic problem-solving solutions. First, the city established a parking management system that nearly eliminates the need to ride around block after block looking for parking. Together with ample parking, parking signage and parking meters aid in keeping drivers informed about parking locations. Second, the city set up a trolley system to transport people around the downtown. This resulted in reducing the need for a car in the downtown, thus also reducing traffic. Pasadena, California, instituted variable meter rates, which, in turn, resulted in having street parking available at all times, even though premium peak rates were charged.

Reducing downtown traffic can be aided by instituting a parking management system that includes meters, signage, valet parking and variable meter rates, so that circling the block is eliminated. Trolleys, and other forms of mass transit, are important to transport not just the customers from one end of the downtown to the other, eliminating the necessity to drive to another location, but also to transport restaurant and retail workers from more remote employee parking lots to their place of employment.

Rising Rents

Another unintended consequence of successful reinvention is the impact that it has on rents in the city. Often, rents are rising in housing and commercial spaces, and, while the taxing authorities are benefiting from increased revenues, the higher rents are pricing some residents and new businesses out of the market. The next cycle of reinvention must consider these issues to avoid an exodus of residents and businesses to more affordable locales. One solution may include zoning code changes that encourage a balanced mix of uses. This will stabilize the parking requirements which impact the cost of construction and associated rents. Similarly, with rising land costs for residential projects, allowing higher densities and increased height will help lower the average unit cost of building residential.

Work on Enhancements

Once a city reaches a degree of reinvention success, it is important to begin thinking about enhancements. Many enhancements involve the public

Calle Mayor. Madrid, Spain

realm, including art in public places, urban parks, enticing gateway features, better lighting, more convenient parking, and wider sidewalks, to name a few. Enhancements, such as public art, deliver a strong message to visitors, residents, office workers and businesses that the city is cultured and offers varied experiences. In a downtown where parking in a garage may be several blocks from a destination, interesting walkability is a must. Think Fifth Avenue in Manhattan where walking five or more blocks to a destination is the norm.

Many European cities, such as Barcelona and Madrid, are reinventing their streets by closing them to cars and opening them to pedestrians only. While logistics, such as deliveries must be addressed, the retailers and restaurants along such pedestrian streets all benefit from the substantial increase in foot traffic and street level activity. American cities are not eager to close streets, especially because early attempts to do so were often not successful. It is time, however, to take a look at the closed street concept again. Turning an automobile street into a pedestrian street is a bold and innovative solution to traffic congestion.

Events

In a reinvented city, improved event venues and special event marketing are magnets for bringing countless residents and visitors to the events. We have already seen how Delray Beach saw the impact of "Art and Jazz on the Avenue." We also saw how West Palm Beach has seen the dramatic effect of its reimagined waterfront, Great Lawn and the Lake Pavilion. Special events both enhance the sales of retailers and restaurants during the event, and provide a memory for its attendees that influences a return visit to the area for both shopping and dining.

An unintended consequence of reinvention, however, is staging too many events and allowing private events that divert revenues from the bricks and mortar retailers and restaurants. These private events are not designed to assist the merchants with sales; rather, they assist the sponsor of the event. Increased traffic congestion and the need for more security often occur as well. These consequences require a candid review and may, ultimately, require a decision by the city to simply issue less permits for private events.

Recognize Transition

Every city goes through transitions. Delray Beach, after the end of World War II, transitioned as new shopping centers emerged and the urban population moved to the suburbs.

Neighborhoods in Manhattan, such as the East Village, SOHO, and Chelsea, transitioned from industrial and clothing manufacturing neighborhoods into areas for young adults, students, artists, the unemployed-creative class, inexpensive cafes, edgy art galleries, and small dot.com businesses. Atlantic Avenue in Delray, lower King Street in Charleston, and Clematis Street in West Palm Beach have transitioned from cheap-chic to national chains. The first wave of the younger population of ten years ago is now older, and some of these people have been replaced by wealthier residents who eat at more expensive restaurants. The older, blighted neighborhoods of these cities are now experiencing the new artsy transition: Delray Beach

(Pineapple Grove District), West Palm Beach (Northwood) and Charleston (Upper King Street). In the dynamics of a reinvented city, leaders and their team of implementers must keep an eye on transitions and the potential impacts, both positive and negative.

Think Big

Now that you face the enviable task of visioning for the next reinvention cycle, it is time to think big. No idea is too immense to consider. You already know how to create the vision, identify the leader, assemble the team, develop a plan, implement the plan, engage the private sector, finance the plan and start the reinvention cycle again!

SOME CONCLUSIONS

The previous chapters have explained the eight-step process of reinventing a city, starting with a vision and ending after some twenty-five years with successful implementation, and then starting all over again with reinvention. Reinventing a city takes a vision, a leader, a plan and a team to implement the plan. There is a process and it can be interrupted at any time if the vision changes, the leader becomes ineffective, the plan is abandoned, or the implementation team dissolves. The hypothesis we have posed is why some cities, such as Bilbao, Charleston, The Hague, West Palm Beach, Delray Beach, and others were able to turn their cities into exciting, livable, financially successful urban centers where people of all ages want to live, work and enjoy life, while other cities just cannot get off the starting blocks.

Each city mentioned here had their own unique approach and set of circumstances. Bilbao was led by a regional cooperative effort and a charismatic mayor who kept the political groups together. Charleston was steered by one man who led it all. West Palm Beach had several visionary mayors who were true leaders. Can elected officials learn how to lead? We believe so; but they need the ability to resist being adversely swayed by naysayers and special interests.

We also know that a leader may emerge from an unexpected arena. It will not always be the charismatic mayor we have seen in so many cities. It may be a citizen who champions historic preservation. It may be a civic organization that sees reinvention as its cause. It can even be a bureaucrat who sees the city through that innovative lens.

The Future of Cities

Many cities in America have dramatically changed in the past twenty-five years as evidenced by our examples of Charleston, West Palm Beach, Delray Beach and others. In the next twenty-five years, there will more changes. Millennials are attracted to exciting urban cores and are flocking to downtowns where there are coffee houses, wine bars, a variety of food, and trendy urban housing, all within walking or biking distance from each other. As the professional labor force moves to the city, companies that depend on this creative class will have to reconsider their office locations. Office buildings in the suburbs are becoming relics of the past; urban offices are the future. Commuting is becoming a waste of time, resources and money. Millennials want to walk or bike to work. Look at the current situation in Amsterdam and The Hague—80 percent of their workforce bikes to work.

As the residents of the urban core decide to walk, bike or take transit to work, the effect on the automobile is evident. We can reduce the number of parking spaces in the downtown and keep a sufficient amount to accommodate residents and visitors who still rely on their cars and are willing to pay to park. Big box retail will shift from a suburban philosophy to a more urban approach. Online retailers, such as Amazon, will affect the need for commercial space. Online taxi services, like Uber and Lyft will affect the need for cars and change the vehicle for hire model.

Active retirees are making their impact on the housing and retail markets known. Many will choose an urban lifestyle in a city's downtown over the gated, golf course community in the suburbs. Boomers and millennials will coexist in the downtowns of tomorrow.

An increasing need for affordable and workforce housing will challenge most cities. Creative approaches to solving this dilemma will be required.

Reinvention efforts that have been primarily applied to a city's urban core will have to be initiated in a city's suburban areas. As more residents and businesses reject the suburban model, the same exodus that harmed downtowns will occur in the suburbs.

Some Conclusions   141

Traditional shopping malls will become less and less viable. New "lifestyle" malls, now being built, attempt to replicate traditional downtowns. These malls, which typically house chain-store consumer goods and clothing, will continue to compete with the eclectic, unique shops emerging in the urban core.

Urban schools, including charter schools, are beginning to pop up in the downtowns as the local school boards react to the future. Reliance on suburban schools will change as well. Urban schools will reopen and be upgraded. School boards will catch up and start building new schools in the downtown. And, because of the lack of available sites, schools may now have to be mid-rise structures.

The future for universities and community colleges will change in the next twenty five years, too. The bucolic campuses of Harvard and Yale will not change, but as the cities of Cambridge and New Haven change, their campuses will become more urban, much like Columbia University's campus, which has become more and more integrated into the New York City grid. Classes now taught online will eliminate the need to commute, except to attend a graduation ceremony. Universities are already decentralizing and this trend will continue. Several of the commuter colleges in South Florida, such as Florida International University, Florida Atlantic University, Broward College, and Dade College, are building in many other cities outside of their central campus. Like Columbia University in New York City, Dade College is almost completely integrated into downtown Miami grid. Palm Beach Atlantic University is entirely integrated in the City of West Palm Beach grid.

Campus housing will follow the moves by colleges and university and the availability of locations for such housing will continue to be an issue.

Our final conclusion is simple: whatever the changes, whatever the issues, every city has the ability to turn itself around. Following the eight steps to reinventing your city takes tenacity, patience and courage. Your efforts, however, will be richly rewarded. Your reinvention may result in the next "CityPlace" or the next "Puppy" or something no one has yet imagined. The possibilities are endless and your city's reinvention can begin today.

CASE STUDIES

Case Study: Bilbao, Spain

Population: 354,000 residents (2013)

Redevelopment Areas: Abandoibarra (Downtown), Ensanche (financial district), Casco Viejo (Old Town), the Nervion River and its banks, Zorrotzaurre (an 84-hectare peninsula in the Nervion River west of downtown) and multiple neighborhoods.

Crisis: The early signs of a crisis occurred in 1973, during the world oil supply crisis and recession. Unemployment then peaked in 1985, at 25 percent, and the city population experienced a dramatic decline—a drop of 70,000 people or 16 percent between 1980 and 1995. In 1985, unemployment of the younger residents reached 50 percent. The various levels of government in the Basque country, including the national government, the autonomous regional government (Pais Vasco), the provincial government (Bizkaia), and the city government (Ayuntamiento) recognized that Bilbao was in a state of crisis with unemployment of 25 percent and the loss of 47 percent of its manufacturing jobs. The unemployment rate persisted for over ten years. The governments jointly set out to make a plan.

Redevelopment Period: 1991–present

Unemployment Rate: 1985–25 percent; 2015–10 percent

144 Reinventing Your City

Guggenheim Museum, Nervion River, University Duesa and University of the Basque Country. Bilbao, Spain

Jill Galarza, Chris Brown, Mayor Areso, and Kim Briesemeister. Bilbao, Spain

Leadership: Leadership came from many organizations and individuals during the regeneration period between 1985 and the present, including the central government (Madrid), the Pais Vasco autonomous region, the Bizkaia provincial government, and the Ayuntamiento (City of Bilbao). At the city level, effective mayors included Josu Ortuondo (1991-1997) and Iñaki Azuna, (1999-2014); effective civil servants included Deputy City

Guggenheim Museum, Nervion River, University Duesa and University of the Basque Country. Bilbao, Spain

Manager Ibon Areso, Director of Metropoli-30 Alfonso Martinez (see below), Director of Bilbao Ria 2000 Pablo Otaola (see below), and others.

Current Leadership: Mayor Ibon Areso, 2014-present

Executive Implementers: Deputy Mayor Ibon Areso; Director of Bilbao Ria 2000 Pablo Otaola (see below)

Vision: As early as the late 1980s, the governments, together with several key consultants, including KMPG, began to articulate a clear vison of transforming the city from a manufacturing and industrial complex (smelting iron ore, steel fabrication, shipbuilding, machine tool manufacturing) to a service industry featuring knowledge-based industries, education, tourism, culture, and finance. In essence, Bilbao had to completely rebuild its economic infrastructure, although it did have pieces in place that served as a launching pad for the expansion of new modern industries.

Plan: The city produced several plans, the first of which was the "Strategic Plan for the Revitalization of Metropolitan Bilbao" (1991), which was also described as the "Master Plan of Bilbao." Key objectives of the master plan included attracting the high-tech sector, implementing inner-city urban renewal, cleaning the Nervion River, cleaning and recycling the Nervion River banks for redevelopment in areas called Abandoibarra, Zorrozaurre peninsula,

Metro Bilbao. Bilbao, Spain. Norman Foster, architect

Baracaldo and others, and establishing a cultural identity. The first plan did not include urban design or specific site planning. Other plans followed. In 1992, the City of Bilbao awarded a design competition for the redevelopment of the downtown, Abandoibarra, to American architect Cesar Pelli. The plan received mixed responses, mainly because it very aggressively featured a series of very tall high-rises alongside the river that would contain retail, residential and office. By the mid-1990s, the planning efforts produced many more plans. The concept of rebuilding the transit system to move rail lines (formerly used to transport iron ore to the smelting plants) away from the river bank, add an extensive regional metro system, and add more stations and lines to the local at-grade street cars was in full swing. The transit vision included linking all the small cities along the river to the center of Bilbao, making the area one cohesive regional city, rather than a series of small, isolated villages.

Beginning in 1992 and for the next twenty years, Bilbao built an extraordinary number of large and architecturally high-profile projects, including a new airport (Calatrava), a new seaport, a new Guggenheim Museum

Iberdrola public multinational electric utility company HQ. Bilbao, Spain

(Gehry), a new metro (Foster), the new Euskalduna Conference Center (Soriano and Palacios), new riverfront parks, new bridges (Calatrava) connecting both sides of the river (which were previously not well-connected because of shipping), expansion of two universities—University of the Pais Vasco and the Duesto University (Raphael Moneo), new corporate headquarters for the utility company, Iberdrola (Cesar Pelli), residential tower blocks (Arata Isozaki), a new Melia Hotel (Ricardo Legorreta) and the list goes on and on.

Key Redevelopment Sub-Organizations: Metropoli-30, created in 1991, and Bilbao Ria 2000, created in 1992.

Finance Partners: Spanish Government, regional Pais Vasco Autonomous Government, Bizkaia Provincial Government, and the City of Bilbao. Also included as an important partner was the Bilbao Ria 2000, a public/public partnership that provided funds from the sale of land in Abandoibarra. The railroads played an equally important role since they owned a large area alongside the river that was later used for redevelopment sites after the railroads were rebuilt in new locations or underground.

Redevelopment projects during the past twenty years include the following partial list: Guggenheim Museum (1997, $200 million), Nervion riverfront parks (1995–2010, $300 million), metro and rail system (1995-present, $2 billion+), conference center and Concert Hall (1999, $159 million), river environmental clean-up (2005, $1 billion), Iberdola Office Tower (2011, $250 million), airport (2000, $70 million and 2015 expansion,

Alfonso Martinez Cearra. Director of Metropoli-30. Bilbao, Spain

$150 million), football stadium (2013, $260 million), and numerous bridges that connected the two sides of the Nervion River.

New Industry: tourism (1 million visitors annually to Guggenheim), cruise ships, technology, port, service, cultural, and education (University of the Basque Country).

Implementation Summary: Bilbao, after the industrial revolution in Europe, became an important center for shipbuilding and manufacturing, particularly steel production, peaking in the mid part of the Twentieth Century. Its river, the Nervion, was not only the dumping site for both industrial and domestic waste, but also the shipping lane for importing iron ore from the province of Asturias and shipping finished steel products to other parts of the world. After the steel mills shut down, unemployment rose from 2.6 percent in 1975 to an intolerable 25 percent in 1985. The city began to lose population. The city quickly became a forgotten wasteland, until new political leadership emerged and a vision to overcome the crisis of high unemployment and the loss of more than 47 percent of the city's manufacturing jobs was created.

The vision and the resulting series of plans came in stages, interspersed with starts and stops. The first was produced in 1985, and was called the *Strategic Plan*. This is when the city realized it needed a plan to counter high unemployment and population loss it was experiencing. An additional plan emerged in 1989, The *Master Plan of Bilbao*. The 1989 plan had an emphasis on the area of the old port of Abandoibarra. Again in 1992, a design competition, won by Cesar Pelli, suggested a series of very tall office and residential buildings on the river in Abandoibarra—an area of 340 hectares. The setting up of a redevelopment agency—Bilbao Ria 2000—was the most important component of the planning effort.

In 1991, the redevelopment team created an organization called Metropoli-30. Its purpose was to act as a facilitator to carry out the strategic plan. Its model was to attract private investment and arrange public/private partnerships. Its focus, in conjunction with Bilbao Ria, was to attract the high-tech, knowledge sector to guide inner-city urban renewal, to support cleaning the Nervion River, to assist with redeveloping the old riverside industrial land in an area called Abandoibarra, and establish a cultural identity, or brand, for the city.

Bilbao Ria 2000 was established in 1992 as a public/public partnership of the governments and public agencies, including the Port of Bilbao and the public railroads. It operates as a quasi-public agency, a planning body in charge of urban redevelopment. Land ownership of the docks in Abandoibarra was transferred to the quasi-public company and valued at zero. Land sales for projects including office and residential towers, retail centers and other private projects were used by Bilbao Ria to fund environmental clean-up, build public parks, install new utility infrastructure, fund art in public places, and beautify the Nervion riverfront. Although the dramatic rise in land value created new private funds for projects, the public sectors contributed significant funds to build the airport, the metro, the convention center, and the Guggenheim. Bilbao Ria's importance as a unified body with considerable authority in urban redevelopment was extremely effective in producing results in the downtown.

Nervion Riverfront. Bilbao, Spain

Its autonomous authority, only requiring a vote of approval by its board of directors, bypassed the bureaucracy of local and regional governmental processes. After great success in the downtown, the agency is currently focusing on following the same approach with the less-affluent riverbank neighborhoods and additional commercial riverbank property.

In the early 1990s, as a result of discussions about making Bilbao a cultural destiny, the Guggenheim Bilbao Museum was conceived somewhat accidentally. In the early '90s, the New York Guggenheim had an exhibit at the Prado Museum in Madrid. A contingent from Bilbao, in particular from the provincial government, visited the Prado with the idea that it would invite the Guggenheim to Bilbao to stage a show of its collection. What ensued eventually was a discussion about the New York Guggenheim's desire to build a new Guggenheim museum in Europe. Over the next year, the museum narrowed the contestants to Salzburg, Austria, and Bilbao. Bilbao won the prize after other European cities showed little interest, and Salzburg suggested that the museum be underground. The downtown location of the future museum in Bilbao was settled, as was the selection of the architect, Frank Gehry. Undoubtedly, the Guggenheim had a major impact on the downtown and the image of Bilbao. In fact, it became an international brand for the city. It represents the revitalization of downtown Bilbao, and it had a further impact because of its proven and consistent record of visitors—close to 1 million annually—and of spurring tourism and the luxury hotel industry in the downtown. It is said to have created 3,800 new jobs in the museum itself, plus the hotel and food and beverage industry, as well as apparel retail shops on Bilbao's main fashion district. The museum was completed in 1997. It became an overnight success. Mayor Ibon Areso remarked in an interview that the Guggenheim really did not want to build in Bilbao, and the Bilbao citizens were really not interested in the American museum coming to Bilbao. But the leadership of Bilbao forged ahead, knowing that the building of a cultural facility of such fame would have great economic development impact.

The City of Bilbao created two redevelopment agencies—Surbrisa in 1985 and Lan Ekintza in 1998—to intervene in several parts of the city, but with different approaches. Surbrisa's objective was to assist inner-city neighborhoods with a concentration of social and housing problems. The crisis at the time was caused by the floods of 1983 that heavily damaged several historic riverfront neighborhoods. The neighborhoods included Casco Viejo (16,000 residents) and Bilbao La Vieja (14,000 residents). However, the funds available for redevelopment were dependent upon contributions from the city, the European Union and the Province of Bizkaia. Lan Ekintza is a city-wide agency promoting business attraction, employment for Bilbao's residents, and job training. Its funding is derived from the city, Bizkaia, Pais Vasco, and the EU. The agency works together with Metropoli-30. Its success rate has been good, averaging 2,000 jobs annually.

Both the crisis of the loss of Bilbao's principal steel making industry and the resulting loss of jobs and population, as well as the end of the dictatorship of Franco in 1975, laid the stage for focusing on a solution to a dysfunctional city in crisis. New energy resulted from being free from the dictatorship and receiving from the national government the authority to become an autonomous state—Pais Vasco. New leadership emerged, having been dormant for over thirty-five years. Between the middle of the 1970s and the 1980s, the city led an effort to write the first strategic plan.

Reinvention: After twenty-five years of redevelopment, Bilbao, partially because of the recession, is analyzing its progress. It is reassessing its successes and failures and is planning for the next twenty-five years. Mayor Ron Areso, the architect of the original plan, together with the futurist Alfonso Martinez, the director of Metropoli-30, and other leaders are thinking about the next phase of reinvention. Bilbao cannot stop at this point. It needs to move forward to another level. The futurist, Alfonso Martinez, suggests the following: Transform the Universidad de Pais Vasco into an international center of learning, particularly changing the emphasis on being a Basque university into one that has world wide appeal, focusing on attracting industry and creative professionals in the high-tech sector, and continuing the resurgence of cultural facilities.

Case Studies 153

Park near Guggenheim Museum. Bilbao, Spain

Playground near Guggenheim Museum. Bilbao, Spain

Case Study: Charleston, South Carolina

Population: 128,000 residents (2013)

Redevelopment Areas: Charleston did not formalize any specific redevelopment district as many cities do, such as when they create a tax increment financing district or a business improvement district. However, the redevelopment projects that have been implemented over the last four decades have been specific buildings, blocks, streets, neighborhoods and specific areas of importance. The areas of regeneration include King Street and Meeting Street (the main streets), the downtown commercial area, historic neighborhoods on the peninsula adjacent to downtown, the College of Charleston campus, Marion Square (the downtown's main plaza), the port, the South Carolina Aquarium, and the Waterfront Park. Outside of the city's downtown, the city rebuilt its airport, and its neighbor to the north, North Charleston, built a convention center (across the river from downtown Charleston).

Crisis: The early signs of a crisis occurred in the 1960s and long before as a result of a general economic malaise, a slow decline ever since the end of the Civil War. The city was in the doldrums, lacked eye appeal, energy and activity.

Waterfront park. Charleston, South Carolina

The downtown main street, King Street, in 1970 contained many vacant buildings, and most buildings had not been renovated since their construction.

In the city election in 1975, however, a new mayor arose from the malaise, and for the next four decades, Joseph Riley steered his vision and redevelopment plan. A second crisis occurred in 1989 during the Riley administration. This was the devastation of the city by Hurricane Hugo. Without hesitation, the mayor continued his plan of redeveloping downtown, preserving historic buildings, and building parking garages (that looked like historic buildings). The city's culinary phenomenon emerged with one successful restaurant after another, and the port built a small cruise ship industry. Much of the downtown retail was repositioned on its main streets, and several important public projects were built, including saving and renovating the historic county courthouse. Riley and his staff attracted hotel developments, both small bed-and-breakfast establishments, as well as hotel flags. Billions of dollars from hurricane insurance proceeds flooded into Charleston between 1991 and 1993 and created a boom period, which gave the city a burst of new activity, construction and consumer confidence. The private sector started to invest in projects of their own, including historic renovation of residences, hotels, and retail establishments.

Redevelopment Period: 1976–present

Unemployment Rate: 1975–10 percent; 2014–4.7 percent

Leadership: Leadership came from principally one person, Mayor Joseph P. Riley, Jr., who was elected in December 1975. His prior experience was as a state legislator for six years. His position as mayor was one of chief executive officer under the strong mayor form of government. He was a quiet visionary who often lectured to audiences with his Kodak Carousel slide show. His shows were convincing because he talked from his own experience.

Vision: The vision for Charleston's redevelopment came from Mayor Riley and others that he recruited. He was always intent on discussing ideas with others, including citizens, his workforce of civil servants, and outside experts

Urban residence. Charleston, South Carolina

whom he met professionally and socially. Mayor Riley was interested in ideas and he made a point to meet great planners, idea people and to listen. He knew a good idea when he heard it, and then he adopted it as his own. Upon taking office in 1976, Mayor Riley's vision was to revive King Street and the commercial downtown first, and then follow by working outward to revitalize the historic areas. He was not a trained city planner in the beginning, but soon thereafter he became one and is revered by urban planners across the country. Part of his early vison came from a trip he took to Europe shortly after being elected mayor. Many of his ideas were formulated from European urban cities.

The Plan: Mayor Riley's first task when he entered office in 1976 was to write a redevelopment plan for the downtown, which turned out to be the first of several. This first plan was written by Barton Ashman of Washington, D.C., under Riley's direction, and was adopted in 1977. Later plans evolved as a series of ideas, memos, directives and city legislation that Riley approved and budgeted with the city council. He never again spent city funds on a grand master plan, although he asked the city council to approve the city's "Ten-Year Plan." Riley disliked spending public money on anything except projects. Much of his grand plan for forty years was lodged in his head, and he never stopped thinking about it from day to day or hour to hour. It was an evolving and constantly changing plan designed by a highly creative person. For him, having the plan in his head and making changes as he wished was somewhat easier than relying on a detailed formal plan. The 1977 plan focused on downtown and suggested that the city build a large hotel and conference center with new commercial uses on a five-acre parcel between King and Market Streets.

The Team: Charleston had a team of civil servants, but it was analogous to one general directing a multitude of foot soldiers, with few managers in between. Riley was charismatic to all, including his staff, who enthusiastically carried out every order.

Implementation: The implementation of the first plan, which was adopted in 1977, centered on the development of a large, multi-story, mixed-use project on 5 acres owned by the city. A request for proposals was issued and a developer selected. After a controversial period of protest and lawsuits against a proposed "large," ten-story project, another developer was selected and the project was scaled down to eight stories. Charleston Place was completed in 1986 at a cost of $75 million. It took nine years to finally build part of Mayor Riley's early vision.

Riley was committed to making Charleston a cultural destination, and in 1977, he quickly forged a relationship with the musical heritage of Spoleto, Italy, called Spoleto USA in Charleston. A highly attended music festival is now held in Charleston every year and sponsored by a non-profit organization. Riley's other notable achievements include the Waterfront Park, Marion Square, the Visitor Center on Meeting Street, the renovation of the Charleston Airport, the attraction of a new aquarium and many others.

Another very important project for Mayor Riley was keeping the county courthouse downtown, particularly after the county administrative offices moved to the suburbs. The mayor was successful, and in the process, he saved an important historic courthouse. Note that counties do not always share the same vision as cities, nor do they always understand their importance as partners in city redevelopment. Charleston County's moving its administrative offices outside of downtown to the suburbs is evidence of that.

Mayor Riley and his staff became highly successful business recruiters for the downtown, especially with retailers and hoteliers. The city is now a highly successful tourist destination, and the downtown is full of bed-and-breakfasts and mid-sized hotels. Two new hotels are planned for Upper King Street—one called the Midtown Project (300 rooms) and the other on Meeting Street (200 rooms). Charleston College, once a 500-student, small, private college has developed into an important city anchor today with 11,000 students. The city has become known for its high quality food and restaurant industry, which influenced several culinary educational institutions to provide employment for students and graduates. Charleston is one of the most important centers of new American cuisine in the country. Together with several cultural facilities, including a performing arts center, an aquarium, museums, and art galleries, a visitor never lacks for something interesting to do.

Reinvention: A new era will soon commence with the end of the extraordinary, forty-year career of Mayor Riley. It is now appropriate to consider taking a look at Charleston and to make improvements that were not accomplished in the last forty years—ones that will contribute to Charleston's greatness and economic health. Whatever the new work for Charleston is, it will take another visionary leader, a new plan, and a great implementation team for the city to meet and further its new goals.

Case Studies 159

Downtown garage. Charleston, South Carolina

Historic downtown building. Charleston, South Carolina

Neighborhood street. Charleston, South Carolina

New residential building. Charleston, South Carolina

Charleston fountain at Riverfront Park. Charleston, South Carolina

Case Study: Delray Beach, Florida

Redevelopment Areas: Downtown, African-American commercial and residential community, near-downtown historic commercial and residential neighborhoods, federal highway commercial corridor, and beach area (Atlantic Ocean) commercial and residential neighborhood. These areas contain approximately 2,000 acres.

Crisis: The early signs of a crisis occurred in the early 1980s, after the oil crisis in 1973, credit crunch in 1983, and the disappearance of 500,000 square feet of retail along the one-mile stretch of the main street. The main street in 1984 contained many vacant buildings, including the original, historic downtown K-12 school. In 1984, at an emotional meeting, the city commission called for a study of the crisis. A committee was formed and a study was completed. The crisis was also documented by the fact that taxable values of

Cornell Museum. Delray Beach, Florida

property were plummeting as a result of the abundant number of vacant and blighted buildings.

Redevelopment Period: 1990–present

Unemployment Rate: 1985–15 percent; 2014 - 8 percent

Leadership: Leadership came from many people, especially elected officials, department heads, and local citizen activists, at different times during the redevelopment period. First came Mayor Doak Campbell, who halted a city commission meeting to declare that he was sick and tired of walking from his office to City Hall in a blighted downtown. He said that night as he slammed his fist on the dais, "Let's do something about our town." The mayor and commissioners formed a committee of business leaders to write a vision plan. It was an historic beginning.

The most important early leadership came in 1990, with the election of Tom Lynch, a local insurance executive, as mayor. Although Delray Beach operates under a city manager and commission form of governance, Mayor

Lynch, because of his leadership skills and charismatic character, did, in fact, lead the redevelopment effort to the next level. The early 1990s were the years that the city elected new business-oriented commissioners, and hired a new city manager, new department heads, including a new, business-oriented redevelopment agency director, and a new Chamber of Commerce director. The Delray Beach renaissance began in 1991.

Vision: Mayor Campbell's committee, called the "Atlantic Avenue Task Force," called for a turn-around and suggested three major actions: first, the city should float a $21 million general-obligation bond issue to rebuild the downtown infrastructure; second, the city should rehabilitate the historic school, called Old School Square, into a cultural center; third, the city should create a tax increment financing district, a statutory community redevelopment agency (CRA), to fund future projects in the downtown. The vision plan was simple, and as a result, every one of the objectives were completed over the next ten years. The task force's report is a lesson in the effectiveness of simplicity, and in setting attainable goals.

The Team: After the vision plan was developed in 1984, the hard work began. The redevelopment agency was conceived as the city department in charge of the downtown and economic development. The agency hired a new director in 1991, a professional from the real estate industry. His focus included the following programs: downtown parking, rehabilitation of downtown structures, acquiring land that could be resold to developers for new projects, finding capital for both the agency, as well as for private investors, retail business attraction, and public infrastructure in the main street. In later years, he added downtown housing, small business lending, and significant land acquisition for the purpose of reselling the land to developers for redevelopment. The Delray Beach team included a fully staffed redevelopment agency, a new city planning director, a strong housing director, and other relevant department heads. The redevelopment agency joint-ventured with the Chamber of Commerce and a small taxing district, a downtown development authority, and the city, to form a downtown marketing team.

The downtown marketing team's executive director very effectively managed the downtown as if it were a 1 million-square-foot mall. Promotions and events were extremely effective in attracting new retail to the downtown.

The Plan: In its early years, the redevelopment agency quickly wrote a redevelopment plan (in-house) and began the implementation. The plan called for leveraging its tax increment to float revenue bonds, which would be used for various programs, such as parking, land acquisition, streetscape, building renovation, and small business lending. The plan was straightforward and contained an important five-year budget. It became the equivalent of a private sector business plan.

Implementation For more than twenty years, Delray Beach has been a model for redevelopment. Its success is derived from good political leadership, a great team of implementers, a good but simple plan, and sound financing. The first phase of implementation, between 1991 and 2000, focused on several principles. First, the agency focused on a small area of their district, the downtown, so that the falling tax revenue would be reversed and could start paying for future redevelopment. Second, the agency focused on

City Oyster & Sushi Bar. Delray Beach, Florida

business recruitment, with emphasis on one use—restaurants. Restaurants, the agency believed, were the catalyst to bring people to the street, and once restaurants consistently located on the street, other retail categories would want to join. Over twenty-five restaurants were brought to Atlantic Avenue, the city's main street. Clustering of these restaurants on one street resulted in a powerful attraction. In the late 1990s, the first women's apparel stores began to arrive. Today, the city is full of women's apparel and beauty services, such as hair, spa, nails, yoga, Pilates and pedicure salons. There are now over 100 restaurants in the downtown, and the city has become a regional draw. Art retailers were introduced in the early 2010s. The city now is known as a cultural center and it is full of public and private theater and music venues, as well as art galleries and private artists' studios. During the first period of 1991-2000 and the second from 2000 to the present, the redevelopment agency, together with the city, focused on parking. "If they come, you better have parking," was the motto.

Public/Private Partnerships: The City of Delray Beach is a study in public/ private partnerships. As the redevelopment agency acquired land, it would partner with developers to develop the land into mixed-use projects, either office over retail or residential over retail. Even other agencies of the city got into the partnership mood, including the housing department that recently approved a tax credit, affordable housing project on public land.

Reinvention: Delray is poised for its next reinvention. Several public properties, including a large downtown tennis center, City Hall and other facilities will need to be reinvented. If it wants to preserve its historic single-family neighborhoods, it will need to consider allowing younger households to move into higher density housing along the transportation corridors. Class A office is needed. Over the past twenty-five years, executives of many national companies now live in Delray, but have their offices in neighboring cities. The city will want to take advantage of this opportunity and encourage executives move their offices to where they live.

East Atlantic Avenue. Delray Beach, Florida

Hyatt Place. Delray Beach, Florida

Case Studies 167

Delray Beach Green Market

100-foot Christmas tree. Delray Beach, Florida

Case Study: The Hague, Netherlands

Author's note: While our case studies for the other cities follow a prescribed format which is intended to simply be a recitation of each city's circumstances and the steps taken to turn those circumstances around, we did not follow the same format with The Hague. The Hague case study is more narrative and includes commentary by Max Jeleniewski, the inner city manager we met in The Hague. We thought the narrative style, coupled with Max's input, would enhance this case study and provide additional insight into the city's reinvention.

Overview: The Hague won the title of *"Best City Center in the Netherlands from 2013–2015."* Although less well known than the physically unique city of Amsterdam, this distinctive and splendid city won the title for good reason. What's so captivating about this city is how the people view themselves relative to other parts of the world, and their approach to staying ahead of potential issues that will negatively affect their quality of life. Very practical and logical, they approach growth and issues with clear, concise strategies. They then masterfully market and promote their plans to their residents. The Hague is the perfect dichotomy in many aspects. It's not uncommon to spot the king or queen in the town, but everyday residents are just as fascinated with each other, and they travel over the same territories on their bikes that the monarchy frequents. They are royal, yet they are everyday. They combine administration and politics. They are historical, yet modern. They are both logical and imaginative.

The Hague is known throughout the world as the city of peace and justice. The moniker dates back to 1899 when delegates from twenty-six countries were invited by Russian Czar Nicholas II (a relative of Dutch Queen Wilhelmina) to talk about issues that arise from being a war-torn region. The Hague had already hosted similar conferences and was a neutral country that was easily accessible from land and sea. One outcome of the conference was the establishment of the Permanent Court of Arbitration, which would become the "temple of peace"—a majestic building with

Case Studies 169

Binnenhof, next to the Hofvijver Lake. The Hague, Netherlands

Binnenhof. The Hague, Netherlands

international prestige. Eventually called "The Peace Palace," the construction of the building was primarily made possible by a gift of $1.5 million from the American philanthropist Andrew Carnegie, whose foundation still manages the Peace Palace. The opening in 1913 was one of the milestones in the history of The Hague.

In 2012, the Supreme Council of Nobility officially granted The Hague the right to include the motto "Peace and Justice" (Vrede en Recht) on its coat of arms, because of the city's contribution over the past century to bringing about a world of peace and justice. This was the first time since 1948 that a motto had been conferred on a Dutch city by Royal Decree—a supreme tribute to the efforts of the more than 18,000 people who work there every day to create a world where peace and justice are a matter of course.

The Dutch are very proud of that moniker—and justifiably so—and the city is keen to highlight its profile as an international city of peace and justice, eagerly showing the world everything it has to offer. Having the international courts and tribunals have helped put The Hague on the world map. In one of their publications, *World Class Accessibility*, produced by the Department of Urban Development, their opening page and description is their brand: International City of Peace and Justice. Simply stated, they "want to provide an environment where countries settle their differences in the courtroom, not in the battlefield; a just, a peaceful world." The Peace Palace is perhaps the city's most photographed building. The Hague is also the second location for the United Nations, with New York being the first.

There are now over 130 international institutions and organizations, and 113 embassies and consulates located in the city, compared to half that a decade ago. The fact that so many international organizations working for peace and justice are concentrated there also attracts knowledge, educational and research institutions. This has encouraged many non-governmental organizations (NGOs) to locate here as well. These NGOs focus on a wide range of issues, from international law to security, and from development

Train station. The Hague, Netherlands

cooperation to peace. In addition, the city has a thriving business sector, including Royal Dutch Shell, Siemens Nederland, KPN, ING Real Estate, and Aegon.

From the turn of the century forward, The Hague gradually, but steadily, became more attractive to organizations from around the world, creating growth pressures, particularly on transportation. The vast investment in public transportation is, no doubt, one reason for the private sector attraction to the area.

The international airport of Schipol, a modern gleaming structure, has direct flights to 260 international destinations. The train infrastructure is ultramodern, and high-speed trains leave The Hague to Paris, Marseille or London, with other trains departing to Belgium and beyond. There are plans to have a direct train to Berlin in the coming years. Locally, the intercity train and tram system are efficient and connect the four largest Dutch cities: The Hague, Amsterdam, Utrecht and Rotterdam.

The Hague is constantly investing in its public transportation network. Regional light rail connections continue to grow and over 1 billion euros will be invested by 2020 to upgrade the network further. Getting around by car is also convenient, but not encouraged, and, in fact, the city has been very proactive in "educating" people, especially targeting the young, in how to use bicycles and other public transportation all with the opening statement, "It's healthy."

But The Hague wasn't always this way. As many of our case studies show, it started with a crisis.

The Crisis: Twenty years ago, The Hague was losing buying power to the suburbs. This was the result of many years of decentralization. After World War II, the emphasis was on everything BIG. Big projects, big roads, big plans, and by the 1960's, some resistance began against this type of redevelopment. Once the public sector got involved in a meaningful way, their focus was on social housing, but no public money was going to the commercial side of the equation. With no public sector investment in the commercial realm, no private investment was generated either. By the 1980s, the realization that the city would need private sector investment to thrive hit home. The government couldn't continue to solely focus on social issues and housing. They needed to get the private sector involved, so they turned to the United States for examples. Baltimore Harbor was the initial model they used because of the public/private nature of the project. The concept was not immediately embraced, however, and the city was still "for the people," not "for the developers."

In 1990, the stark reality that something had to be done became apparent. This moved the city to hold a competition and get bids for two main initiatives. The first was to build a new city center in downtown, and the second was to build parking. This was the city's way of placating both the left and the right side of government. The garage was to encourage private sector investment, and the City Hall was for the liberals looking for all things "for the people." A contract, or (development agreement as we call it in America), was drafted between the private investors and the government, and this was cited as the beginning of the change for The Hague.

Backtracking to the late 1980's, the decision to build the city hall where it's currently located and to end the days of BIG roads, was championed by the local politician Adri Duivesteijn. A picture depicting Duivesteijn holding a huge hammer over the equally huge roads with the intent of breaking the roads into pieces signaled the change in investment temperament, with a focus on attracting the private sector. The investment had to be in conveniently located garages and public transportation, not in big roads. Also at the time, all trams were above-ground, and as the city grew denser, altercations between pedestrians and trams began. Max Jeleniewski, the inner city manager we met in The Hague, emphasized the conflict from back then showing pictures of a tram wreck with a car. A civil engineer and urban planner by training, Max spent quite some time sharing the history of The Hague with us, along with his colleague Frans Botma.

The struggle that occurred between factions—the ones who wanted to cater to the social masses versus others who recognized that the private sector needed to be part of the equation—was a difficult one. With Duivesteijn's influence, the new garage and public investment was geared toward private developers, and the new City Hall building was the symbol that the government would still be totally dedicated to the people by providing an iconic public facility. And iconic it is. Richard Meier, an American architect, designed one of the most beautiful, yet functional, public buildings in Europe. Blending into the modern, historical skyline of the city, the building feels modern and fresh, but due to the monochromatic color scheme and stark metal finishes, it looks like it's been hosting residents for a very long time.

By 2005, the new tunnel was completed and the BIG road was put underground. Plans to move the tram system underground began and are still underway today with partial tram systems operating out of the pedestrian's way. With the government now considering what the private sector might want or need to invest, they approached it with typical systematic style. With the new public infrastructure going in, they created a proactive

The Hague skyline

Interior of The Hague City Hall

The Passage. The Hague, Netherlands

approach to dealing with private investment by crafting zoning and land use laws to drive exactly the type of development they wanted. City staffers got creative at negotiating projects when they didn't like "the look" of the building. By agreeing to increase development capacity, developers were prompted to design and build better projects. They started actively recruiting retailers and set up an elaborate economic development system to meet and greet new investment as it arrived. There were policy documents that provided specific rules for development, but the staff was able to blend negotiated design elements and grant variances when warranted.

In fact, Max took great delight in telling us how he holds the government and city buildings to the same standards as any private building.

One of the most difficult aspects of The Hague's redevelopment efforts was effectively combining building elements that are old and new in an older European city. One such project is called "The Passage," which was designed by the architect, Bernard Tschumi. The original building is a stately old building on a street that stretched over a few blocks. The goal was to connect the city center streets where old buildings that couldn't be restored were sitting. Tschumi created an extension of The Passage that cleverly blends old and new. But more importantly, he connected the street grid in a way that opened up a new pedestrian walkway that was sorely needed. It's another example of the emphasis the city places on traffic, transportation and connectivity.

Most of the current plans follow the planning document Binnenstad Den Haag 2010–2020, (Innercity, The Hague 2010–2020). According to Max, the plan, drafted in 2009 as a successor of the 2000–2010 plan, looked at the DNA of each area of the city. The plan calls for what most redevelopment wonks would think are practical redevelopment goals. The approach was for an accessible, clean and safe city. The Dutch and the planners in The Hague take the accessibility part very seriously.

In the plan, The Hague recognizes the city is growing, and there will be more people, more jobs, and more visitors. But they also recognize that, in the last decade, there have been new developments and trends that will affect mobility, including the pursuit of sustainability, climate change or technological developments, such as navigation systems and mobile internet.

"With conscious choice we make an appeal to citizens, visitors and businesses to more consciously think about the mobility and the environment as they choose their mode of transport," Max said. Transportation documents promote that The Hague can and will help by ensuring that there is more to choose from, and it is becoming easier to make the right choice. Smart organization is always a good idea, but it is especially needed when space is scarce. The space to widen roads and construct parking, due to the limited remaining land, must be considered, as well as the environmental impact. The move from car to bicycle or public transport must become more attractive.

So, the plans set policies for 2010–2020 with an outlook toward 2030. The eight policy goals include:

- A sustainable and healthy city
- Reliable access to top locations
- Choosing public transport more often

- More cycling
- Bundling, organizing and integrating car traffic
- Good facilities for pedestrians
- Attractive mobility
- Quiet and spacious residential areas

Obviously The Hague, Amsterdam and other European cities enjoy a bicycle culture that many cities in America may never achieve for many reasons. The sheer numbers are something for us to begin to measure and ask where we can make changes. For example, two thirds of all trips fewer than one kilometer are on foot in The Hague. These are trips to the shops, schools or sports clubs. The Hague's vision of becoming a sustainable and healthy city actually sets a goal of growing bike traffic by 30 percent and public transport by 40 percent. Max told us 46 percent of people either bike or walk as their means of transportation. With that said, there are thirty theaters, twenty-six cinemas, forty-five museums, 4,211 shops, seven markets, 490 restaurants and 363 cafes to visit also!

As noted earlier in the case study, The Hague is a dichotomy as a city. The overall goal is for an accessible, clean and safe city. The emphasis is also very much on the people and what they will be doing in the city. The focus is not only on what will have to happen, but also on how people feel when they're there.

The "calling cards" of The Hague are carefully thought out and specific. These characteristics are their identity in the plan:

- Royal and Everyday
- Administration and Political
- Stately and Elegant
- Historical and Modern
- International and Multicultural
- Music and Dance

Bike parking in a plaza in The Hague, Netherlands

Garage parking showing the number of available parking spaces. The Hague, Netherlands

Max told us that now that the tunnel and transportation efforts are almost complete, and the private sector is flocking to invest in the city, this will extend to other target uses and attractions. In the city of Leiden, a few miles north of The Hague, a thriving university system is in place. The city leaders recognized the need to have younger residents and a more active, around-the-clock environment, and they actively sought out the university. Leiden University will now open a third tower in downtown, with students coming from all over. Student count is reaching 3,000, with more planned for future semesters. This will also support the ambitious goals of additional downtown housing. The cover of one section of the plan translates into "Nearly a Complete City Hague!"

The following article was contributed by Max and details some of the major redevelopment successes in The Hague based on his work as the inner city manager. Note, Max stated the three main reasons that caused the efforts to be successful, were:

1. Government Policies (we called it leadership in Chapter Two)
2. Public Investment (same as initiatives mentioned in Chapters Four and Six)
3. A Professional Team (same as Chapter Three)

"My History of the Inner City of The Hague"
By Max Jeleniewski

In 2013, four big building projects are in progress in the Grote Marktstraat in the inner city in The Hague, the Netherlands. About ten years ago, just after the completion of the tramtunnel and parking garage (360 places) under the street, the idea came up to use the positive vibe in the street to transform it into an "International Shopping Boulevard," instead of a normal shopping street in a normal city. This matched the new ambition of the city to develop the city as the International Capital of Peace and Justice.

Max Jeleniewski. Inner City Manager. The Hague, Netherlands

The local government still had a budget of 12 million euro to finish the pavement and lighting in the street. From a proposal, an architect (Lana du Croq) was selected. Based on the traditional court culture in the city (the former queen and present king live and work in The Hague), she designed a ballroom with corresponding floor and chandeliers. The first new project was a shopping mall combined with a cinema, a fitness center (including a swimming pool) at the top, and a casino. This project was finished in 2007. Subsequently, my team and I decided to meet the main owners of real estate in the street and discussed with them the possibilities for expanding their businesses or to renew their premises. Four new projects came out of this:

The new Passage, as a continuation of the older passage from the Nineteenth Century. This project includes a hotel with 120 rooms. The building is designed by Bernard Tschumi.

The Amadeus, built on a location where Mozart (at the age of ten!) stayed for seven months in 1765 and 1766 and composed about ten works. There are seventy-six apartments and a Primark store of 8,000 m^2. The apartments will be available in 2015 and all the apartments are sold already. The name of the building was an idea of ours.

The Sijthoff complex is being renovated at the moment. The project adds 4,500 m^2 of retail. The facade is a real eye-catcher.

The Markies is a complex with the renewed Marks & Spencer and H&M flagship stores. Recently, the whole project was sold to a German and a Dutch investor for around 100 million euro.

All in all in recent years, 25,000 m^2 was added to the 60,000 m^2 of retail in the shopping boulevard, crisis or no crisis. This is a huge success in the period of recession in Europe in the period 2008-2014. The reason that this happened is because of consequent municipal policies, the previous investments in infrastructure and transportation, and a good investment climate due to a good (and small) team of professionals both in the private and public sector. By July 2015, the street will be finished—both the building projects and the public space.

Hereby, I invite everybody to come to the International Shopping Boulevard in the International City of Peace and Justice!

Max Jeleniewski
Manager Inner City
The Hague, Netherlands

Case Study: Curacao, Dutch Caribbean

Author's note: This case study, like The Hague, follows a narrative format.

Curacao is one of six Dutch territories in the Caribbean—three in the Windward Islands, including Curacao, Aruba (the most well-known to Americans), and Bonaire; and three in the Leeward Islands, including Saba, St. Eustatius and St. Maarten. St. Maarten is shared by the Dutch and French. In order to appreciate the island of Curacao's successful transformation, you have to understand what Curacao went through over the last thirty-plus years. It is one of the best redevelopment stories in all of the Caribbean basin, and a place you MUST visit.

Today, Curacao is a picturesque island with multiple three and four-star hotels and amenities, some of the finest dining in the western hemisphere, striking beaches and some of the best dive locations in the Caribbean. The downtown boasts buildings that are 350+ years old, and some of the most stunning architecture in the world is located on this tiny island of 100,000 inhabitants. The primary language is Dutch, but the island dialect, called Papiamento, is spoken by all the locals and is used in the schools as a main language. English is widely spoken, as is Spanish, and most locals speak a fourth language. The city operates under Napoleon law, and the main industry today is tourism and the port.

The island wasn't always like that, however. But before we get to the island's bigger redevelopment issues, let us frame the day-to-day living challenges. In 1980, the only true semblance of American influence was McDonald's and Kentucky Fried Chicken; hence very few Americans visited the island. The island also lacked everyday conveniences most Americans took for granted. For example, to call family in the United States, one had to call the operator and ask "her" to place the call. A wait of anywhere from one to three hours would ensue, and the operator would call back and say she had family on the line. God help you if you got cut off. TV programming was even trickier. If you wanted to watch something during the eight hours of broadcasting on the sole local channel, (yes only eight hours and only one local channel—it was 1980 after all) the TV host would come on every so often and say, "Such and such program will begin MORE OR LESS at about X time." No one really seemed to see the issue in this programming format; moreover, in most homes, there really wasn't anything akin to a hot water heater. It was an island, after all, and with temperatures hovering around 80 degrees year-round, no one really cared for hot water. But, the plumbers would run the copper water pipes through the roof, and the sun would heat the pipes along with the water in them, so if you wanted a hot shower, you would be sure to take one in the afternoon; otherwise you were going to get cool or tepid water. We're sure our Dutch friends who read this are rolling their eyes and thinking how spoiled we Americans are to even mention such island idiosyncrasies. And, they are right. Just for clarification, these situations were commonplace on most islands, not just "Dushi Korsow," which is translated as "Sweet Curacao." Today, the island enjoys all the modern conveniences one could want.

Life back then, however, was calm and simple with people paying attention to what should matter most—family, time together, enjoying nature and everyday experiences. As described previously, however, redevelopment changes places and progress is usually important.

Things have drastically changed on this charming island, and most of the American conveniences are commonplace now. A wholesale change in investment attitudes happened and money is finding Curacao.

In the 1980s, Aruba, Curacao's sister island, had all the big name hotels and catered to Americans. Even though Curacao was the capital, it largely had to rely on the many Venezuelans and the few European (mainly Dutch) tourists in the summer to support the island.

It took a crisis for the island to wake up and face the critical situation it was in. In 1969, some political renegades tried to burn down the downtown. Between then and 1980, not much had happened, and Curacao's residents were quite complacent. If tourists came, so be it, if they didn't, that was fine too. There was an offshore agreement with the United States, and in the mid-1980s the agreement ended. The large, offshore business that once flowed freely through the island dried up! Major blows hit the island all at once. Fortune 500 companies that went through Curacao (due to the minimum offshore taxation) to fund and finance themselves in the European markets stopped. The hundreds of millions of dollars that flowed through the offshore companies had been a lifeline of income for the government.

The second blow came when the Venezuelan currency, the Bolivar, crashed and was devalued so quickly that the downtown went into a recession almost overnight. Venezuelans, who used to come to Curacao by the planeloads and shop for the duty free and European brands they could not get at home, suddenly stopped coming. These same tourists also loved to gamble, so the casinos and hotels also took a hit. The final blow came when the island's Shell Oil refinery closed. Once a portal for Venezuelan oil, the shuttering of the refinery caused the loss of hundreds of jobs. There was suddenly no tourism, no major employer, and no revenue to the government

Aerial view showing the downtown in the front and the refinery in the background. The waterway leads to the port. The floating bridge (connecting the two sides) opens to allow cruise ships to slice through the center of town and dock near the shops. Curacao

Case Studies 185

The floating bridge literally "floats" on large pontoons. It opens for ships but is mainly used for pedestrians to cross from one side of town to the other. Curacao

The famous and picturesque "Handelskade" along the waterway in downtown Punda.

from outside. Talks included rhetoric about some malcontents burning the town down once again.

Don Werdekker was the secretary of the Chamber of Commerce at the time and the Chamber was a very powerful business force on the inland. Per Napoleon law, chambers of commerce require the mandatory registration of all businesses and companies. Every year, businesses pay an amount based on the company's capital and, although the fee may be deemed nominal, like our business tax receipts in the States, it adds up. In the U.S., that money goes to the cities and is called a business license or business tax. Under Napoleon law, such as in Curacao and much of Europe, the chambers get the money to advocate for business wants and needs. They monitor regulations and how the regulations may affect the business economy, they hold formal functions related to all things business, and they lobby against taxation or other non-business-friendly efforts by the government.

Leadership: Don was part of a group of very influential leaders that knew something had to be done and quickly. The Curacao Action Group (CAG) was formed and was headed up by Ron Gomez Cassares. He was bright and forward-thinking, as well as likeable and influential. His day job was vice president of the largest bank on the island, Maduro and Curiels Bank. Other members of the CAG were representatives from the most prominent industries, including the refinery, the hotel industry and other economic institutions, as well as several wealthy and influential members of the business community.

The Plan: The CAG knew they needed support from outside consultants and hired Arthur D. Little, a consulting firm out of Boston, Massachusetts. Completed in 1985, the plan made recommendations on three main sectors for the government: 1) tourism, with the focus on the historic downtown; 2) "logistics," or all things that affect the functioning of the island, such as trade, economics, the harbor and deep-water port, transshipping large vessels going into the free zone, etc.; and 3) investment in projects.

Downtown and Tourism: Even though the plan outlined recommendations, the issues were so vast and deep within each of the three sectors, more detailed plans were needed to have enough depth to ensure the plans would be successful. The downtown was an old historic district with beautiful buildings over 350 years old. The historic preservation group out of Holland that monitored the structures was not going to let anything happen to those buildings, so when an American firm was hired that specialized in "festival marketplaces," which were all the rage in the '80s, the leaders knew they would have to make sure the plan respected the current conditions and not resort to standard Americanized solutions. CAG hired Trahan, Burden and Charles, and Sandy Hillman of the firm, was deployed to the island to deal with the failing retail industry and to increase tourism.

Again, the trend of 1980 was to create a festival marketplace in downtowns, but there was no way to start from scratch in Curacao. Having just worked on the Inner Harbor project in Baltimore, Sandy was excited to reinvent that concept. So, as the team was driving to the hotel, as they crossed over a very high bridge and looked down at the downtown, everyone saw the same thing at the same time and, according to Don's recollection, Sandy exclaimed, "We don't have to build it, it's already here!!" What they saw was the 400-year-old abandoned fort with cannon holds, artillery portals and all, overlooking the Caribbean ocean! The fort was called the Waterfort Arches (the Waterfort Bogges) and was used to house the military and prisoners in the early days. The fort sat right on the edge of the downtown, and could act as a catalyst for the city center. Once the overall downtown tourism plan was devised, the next stage would be to make sure it would get implemented.

Just having the downtown plan wasn't enough. Now they needed an implementation plan, so they found one of the best retail marketers with tourism experience in the United States, Carolyn Feimster. Carolyn had a tremendous retail marketing background and worked tirelessly with Bill Fothergill from Arthur D. Little and Sandy Hillman from TBC to make sure the right formula was in place for implementation that would have a broader impact than just one section of downtown.

Consider the layers: First, came Arthur D. Little, who then hired Trahan Burden and Charles, who then hired Carolyn Feimster. It took a considerable length of time, but it also took that many layers of detailed plans to get it done right.

Carolyn wrote the first marketing plan to revitalize the downtown, and she recommended a funding structure, as well as an organizational plan, to oversee the redevelopment efforts. It didn't take her long to notice that Don was the right person to lead the downtown and the island's tourism out of the ashes, but he was already busy running the Chamber of Commerce. The leadership roles at this point were critical for the island to pull itself out of "the mess," so after much thought, Don and the CAG agreed that downtown was so important to the overall island recovery that he should lead the new entity—the Downtown Management Organization (DMO). The general funding was to come from a combination of membership dues from the merchants, the Chamber of Commerce and the government. It was an interesting marriage of financial partners, and "but for" those alliances, the DMO wouldn't have had sufficient funding.

In the meantime, while the downtown was getting organized and systems were being put in place, two other initiatives were also gaining traction. A very strong alliance was forming between the banks, the harbor and trans-shipping industry, the hotel industry and the Curacao International Trade Association (CURINTA), the entity trying to build support for a World Trade Center in Curacao.

Ultimately, the Irish were brought in to assist with the development of the World Trade Center, which got financed and built. The development of the Duty Free Zone was expanded and acted as a stepping stone to South America for imports and exports to go through the island's deep-water port.

Now that the downtown plan had a funding source and management, the efforts turned to very specific actions that would start to revitalize the downtown. The once-spotless streets were now littered and lined with graffiti and trash. Drug addicts owned the European-styled plazas and parks, and merchants were afraid. The third initiative—improving accessibility—was

Case Studies **189**

Historic building downtown, referred to as "The Wedding Cake" building. Curacao

Penha, one of the oldest and the most photographed buildings in downtown Punda.

the one that was probably the most vital to attracting the first breed of new customers to downtown—the locals. The tourists weren't coming yet, and the Venezuelan currency continued to fall. The only way to slowly start the cash registers ringing was to target the limited number of warm bodies on the island and try to get them downtown.

As simple as it sounds, the reason the locals didn't like going downtown was because there was nowhere to park. The government workers took all the spaces. The few spaces that were left, if any, were used by merchants and store employees. Don noted that he was almost lynched when he suggested that the civil servants should park at a central lot down the street, and the merchants thought that was hysterical. Why should they walk when they were there all day?!

Don forged on and established a central parking lot, and then he did the unthinkable—he installed meters, which drove the employees to the central parking, which freed up the most convenient locations for shoppers. The DMO even had to do a promotion to get the merchants to agree to stop parking in the prime spots. Eventually, the system started to work and locals began to drift into town; however, the "clean and safe" issue persisted.

Clean and Safe: The concept of an area being dirty and dangerous is about as certain a retail killer as you can get. Cleanliness is easy to solve if you have funds. Hire guys in nice colored shirts, maybe even call them ambassadors, and have them give directions and offer other advice or smiles, and you start to get clean streets. The DMO had the money, so they hired a few guys, and they started to clean the area up daily. The merchants initially weren't very cooperative themselves, and they would pointedly put their trash out any time of day! At one point, Don went quietly to the government and convinced them to start fining the merchants who put trash out before the stores closed. Problem solved. In the 1980's however, Don noted that drug dealers and homeless people don't like it when you improve an area, and they're usually not timid about saying so in their own ways. Vagrants would come to town at night and were breaking into the stores, as well as terrorizing people

Case Studies 191

The Governor's Palace and central government offices. Curacao

A revitalized retail street in Otrobanda (the other side) of downtown, Curacao

during the day. The island had been in decline for so long, and so many people were out of work, that many resorted to burglary and other crimes. The continuous presence of crime and danger was affecting the kickstart of downtown. Don walked the street day after day, talking to the merchants and trying to get them to contribute to a fund so he could start a security force. Some of the wealthier merchants had their own private security, but it was not very effective. The police were also not effective because there were so few of them. At one point, the DMO rattled the police by calling on them to respond to the break-ins, but the commanding officer apologized and said the patrol officers would call in sick if they had to walk the streets in the daytime (too hot). So without the merchants or the police willing to deal with it, Don tried one last attempt at holding a merchant meeting and showing them how much money they could save from a reduction in theft and an increase in new business if they each just invested a little money (the equivalent of $85 a month) to start a security force downtown. There were no takers.

Then one day something terrible happened.

Kishore Mukki, an Indian merchant who owned a duty-free store, was in his shop at the end of the day. His wife had left for the day and he was closing the store alone. When he didn't come home for dinner, they went looking for him and found him later that night in the back storage area with a wire around his neck, dead.

All hell broke loose and the entire island was up in arms. Every merchant was calling Don and screaming that something had to be done immediately. He pulled out his security concept materials and told them what he had been telling them for over a year—they had to join together and invest in a security team to make the downtown a safe place to be. Most of the merchants finally relented, and Curacao Hospitality Services (CHS) was formed. Headed by a former Dutch police officer who knew how to deal with the criminal element, CHS began to attack the crime problem. CHS hired men who were trained in security tactics, but who also presented a friendly demeanor to the general public with their dress code, so as to not

Boat launch for the small fishing vessels that go out daily for fresh catch, Curacao

signal the need for a huge security presence. The major criminal activity halted almost overnight. Burglars were getting caught and thrown in jail, and the drug addicted population moved to quieter areas away from the town center.

Once the basic elements of making the downtown a place people would want to go to were in place, the other elements of marketing and merchandising and tourism promotion started. Don went on to head the Curacao Hospitality and Tourism Association (CHATA) as the island's tourism czar. Working closely with the public sector Tourism Board, Curacao gradually witnessed a major influx of hotel investment to the island. His continued and tireless commitment to improving the economics of the island over a thirty-year period resulted in the incredible honor by Queen Beatrix of the Dutch Kingdom of conferring knighthood upon Don. Don is now entitled to be called Sir Don!

The cruise ship industry was picking up, thanks to the CAG and the Chamber, and the other sectors of the island were slowly growing. By 2004, multiple three and four-star hotels had opened, and private investment was flooding in. Americans who were familiar with Aruba started to venture over to Curacao. Other major investments on the island were also taking place.

Today, the island is a safe and beautiful place for visitors. Downtown is thriving and business is robust, although it is still an island with lots of competition. What the island has done, however, is take all the pieces from the original plan and continue on a steady and positive growth path. The island always had far more natural beauty with its historic buildings and other assets and amenities than neighboring Aruba and other islands; it just needed them to be promoted. The private sector had to find and then invest in the island, which it has now done in a meaningful way. Now, Curacao has the best of everything, including shopping, hotels, diving, tourism, international performances, and more, the tourism numbers are skyrocketing and people are discovering what has been there all along.

Going Forward The next decade will be very important for this island. A new major shopping mall is planned not far from the airport. The goal is to target and attract the South American tourists who currently fly to Miami. The impact on the south Florida market will be hard to measure, but the influx of that much retail on the island will clearly affect the downtown and other retail areas on the island. Downtown must stay vigilant and progressive. The American mall concept is not one that necessarily fits in all environments (see Bilbao case study). Curacao has been through rough times before, and hopefully will no doubt emerge better than ever.

This is one island you MUST visit.

Look for Curacao tourism information at www.curacao.com

BIBLIOGRAPHY

Interviews
Note: Dates indicate the year of interview.

West Palm Beach, Florida
Lois Frankel, Congresswoman, 22nd Congressional District Florida, and former Mayor of West Palm Beach, 2014

Nancy Graham, former Mayor, West Palm Beach, 2014

Jeri Muoio, Mayor, West Palm Beach, 2014

Kenneth Himmel, President and CEO, Related Urban, New York, 2014

Rick Greene, Development Services Director, City of West Palm Beach, Florida, 2015

Raphael Clemente, DDA Director, West Palm Beach, Florida, 2015

Delray Beach, Florida
Cary Glickstein, Mayor, Delray Beach, 2014

Jeff Perlman, former Mayor, Delray Beach, 2014

Doak Campbell, former Mayor, Delray Beach, 2014

Tom Lynch, former Mayor, Delray Beach, 2015

Tim Hernandez, Developer, New Urban Communities 2014

Butch Johnson, Restauranteur, Delray Beach 2014

Francis Borque, former Chairman of the Board, Old School Square Foundation, 2015

Pompano Beach, Florida

Lamar Fisher, Mayor, Pompano Beach, 2014

Dan Hobby, Historian, Pompano Beach, 2014

Dennis Beach, City Manager, Pompano Beach, 2015

Charleston, South Carolina

Joseph P. Riley, Mayor, 2014

Christopher Morgan, AICP, Director, Planning and Neighborhoods Division, 2014

Bilbao, Biskaia, Spain

Anaki Azuna, Mayor, 2013

Ibon Areso, Mayor, 2014

Alfonso Martinez Cearra, General Director, Bilbao Metropoli-30, 2014

Dr. Beatriz Plaza, Professor of Economics, University of Pais Vasco, 2014

Juan Alayo Azcarte, Urban Planner, former Director of Development Planning, Bilbao Ria 2000, 2014

Natxo Tejerine Gonzalez, Urban Planner and Lawyer for the Regeneration of the City of Barakaldo, 2014

Estibaliz Luengo Celaya, Director, Bilbao International, 2014

Eric Britton, Futurist, Development Economist, Managing Director, EcoPlan International, Lyon, France, and Founding Editor, *World Streets*; eric.britton@ecoplan.org

Mikel Murga, Civil Engineer, Lecturer, MIT, 2014

Donald Brackenbush, Urban Planner, Los Angeles, California, 2014

Pablo Otaola, Director Commission for the Restoration of Zorrotzaurre and former Director of Bilbao Ria 2000, 2014

Inaki Duque, Bilbao Ria 2000, 2014

Liu Thai Ker, Chairman, Livable Cities, World Cities Conference; Bilbao, 2013, liu_thai_ker@rsp.sg

The Hague, Netherlands

M. A. Jeleniewski, MScCE, Manager Inner City, City of the Hague, The Hague, 2014

Frans Botma, Engineer, City of the Hague, The Hague, 2014

Don Werdekker, Urban Redevelopment Consultant and former Director of Curacao Hotel and Tourism Association, 2014

Periodicals
General

Haentjens, Jean (2012), "Crises: La Solution des Villes" FYP EditionsBilbao, Spain1.

Plaza, Beatriz (2006) "The Return on Investment of the Guggenheim Museum," International Journal of Urban and Regional Research, Wiley Blackwell

Gomez, Maria V. (1998) "Reflective Images: The Case of Urban Regeneration in Glasgow and Bilbao," Blackwell Publishers

Plaza, Beatriz (2007) "The Bilbao Effect": University Library of Munich, Germany

The Hague, Netherlands

Frans Botma (2014) Cycling in The Netherlands and The Hague: Department of Urban Development/Traffic www.denhaag.nl/binnenstadsplan (2014) Binnenstadsplan Den Haag

Peter Smit—Deputy Mayor (2013) World Class Accessibility; City of The Hague

CREDITS

Alicia Alleyne, Director of Administration, Redevelopment Management Associates, (RMA), Pompano Beach, Florida

Lauri Blake, Contributing Editor

Mark Briesemeister, Contributing Editor

Peter H. Brown, Architect and Director, Better Neighborhoods, Houston, Texas

Estabiliz Luengo Celaya, Interview Coordinator, Bilbao, Spain

Diane Colonna, Delray Beach Community Redevelopment Agency

Edda Danovich, Translator, Bilbao, Spain

Horacio Danovich, Engineer, Pompano Beach, Florida

Gemma Rojo Del Amo, Interview Coordinator, Bilbao, Spain

Marjorie Ferrer, Downtown Delray Beach Development Authority

Elaine Fitzgerald, Beach Vacation Rentals

Jill Galarza, Interpreter and Translator, Bilbao, Spain

Rick Gonzalez, REG Architects, West Palm Beach, Florida

Dan Hobby, Pompano Beach Historical Society, Pompano Beach, Florida

Max Jeleniewski, MScCE, Manager Inner City, The Hague

Dr. Lee Thai Ker, Chairman, Centre for Livable Cities, Singapore

Claudia M. McKenna, Retired City Attorney, City of West Palm Beach, Contributing Editor

Christopher Morgan, AICP, Director, Planning and Neighborhoods Division, Charleston, South Carolina

Don Werdekker, Interview Coordinator, the Hague, Netherlands

Carol Westmoreland, Executive Director, Florida Redevelopment Association

Office of the Mayor, Bilbao Spain

All of the dedicated, passionate and incredibly talented RMA employees

www.flightnetwork.com

www.guggenheim-bilbao.es

www.tripadvisor.com

ABOUT THE AUTHORS

Kim J. Briesemeister and Christopher J. Brown are principals in Redevelopment Management Associates (RMA), a consulting firm that also provides management and staffing services to governments. They formed RMA in 2009 when they recognized that many cities needed professional expertise to deal with the daily issues associated with reinventing their cities.

Christopher J. Brown has had a long successful career in real estate development with several major public companies, including Mitchell Energy and Development (Houston) and Campeau Corporation (Toronto), as well as his own firm (Delray Beach). In1991, Mr. Brown became the executive director of the Delray Beach Community Redevelopment Agency, a tax increment financing district in a Florida seaside town of 50,000 people. Today, Delray Beach is touted as one of the most successful redevelopment stories in the United States, with land values soaring from $10 to over $300 per square foot. His initiation into urban redevelopment began during his educational years at Yale University, followed by the University of Pennsylvania, where he earned dual Masters Degrees in Architecture and Urban Planning. He served as an adjunct professor at Rice University's Architecture and Planning Department. Mr. Brown resides in Delray Beach, Florida.

Kim J. Briesemeister has dedicated her professional career to downtown and city redevelopment, with particular emphasis on helping cities to focus their efforts to get redevelopment started. Creating a realistic vision for an area and forming clear-cut implementation strategies that include public-private partnerships, financing and marketing are a few of her trademark skills. She began her career abroad in the Netherland Antilles, where she learned to operate in an environment with over twenty cultures and nationalities that co-existed in the downtown business district. After over a decade of international experience, she moved back to the United States. She continued to work in the redevelopment field in Florida for various municipalities, including the cities of Hollywood, Fort Lauderdale and West Palm Beach. Her work has resulted in over $750 million in private-sector investment and development. She has been the president of the Florida Redevelopment Association (FRA), Co-Chair of the Alliance Program for the International Council of Shopping Centers (ICSC), and she sits on the Advisory Board for the University of Miami's School of Architecture's Master's in Real Estate Development and Urbanism. She is also a Certified Redevelopment Administrator. Ms. Briesemeister resides in Pompano Beach, Florida, with her husband, Mark.

Redevelopment Management Associates, LLC
954.695.0754
www.rma.us.com
info@rma.us.com